Shock & Awe

The honest reactions and humble
reflections of a sin-prone saint.

A Daily Devotionary On the Psalms of David

KEN MILLER

SHOCK & AWE

ISBN-10: 0692767304
ISBN-13: 978-0692767306

DEDICATION

This is book is dedicated to my six children: Taylor, Maggie, Kate, Molly, Hudson and Mandy. They have each been a major source of encouragement to me over the years and have never failed to provide me with countless illustrations for my lessons and incentive to be in God's Word. Over the years, we read a lot of great books together. And it was the overwhelming responsibility of being a dad that drove me to seek guidance from the Scriptures. They weren't that difficult, but I had a lot to learn about being a father. And while I am still a work in process, learning to be a grandfather as well, I wouldn't trade my role as a dad for anything in the world. Even a best-selling book.

CONTENTS

SHOCK & AWE

ACKNOWLEDGEMENTS

I want to thank all those who have read, commented on, critiqued and even criticized my online blog, vesselsofclay.org, over the years. There have been plenty of mornings when I feared that what I had written had disappeared into the ethernet, never to be seen by any other living human being. But then I would get a text or an email from a faithful follower, sharing their thoughts or, at times, simply their thanks. It was the many words of encouragement that finally got me to take my thoughts and put them into print – in a book. I am grateful for their support. My prayer is that this more traditional medium will reach a different audience altogether, encouraging them to fall in love with the Word of God.

SHOCK & AWE

BEFORE YOU BEGIN

This is the second in a series of "daily devotionary guides." Their purpose is to assist you in the reading and study of God's Word. Unlike most devotionals, this one is designed to use alongside your study of the Bible. In this case, it will take you through the psalms of David. This book is not intended to read in one sitting. Each chapter has been divided into three days. Day One entails you reading the psalm for that day, followed by the corresponding devotionary. On Day Two, you will find a version of the psalm written in my own words. The goal is for you to begin personalizing each day's psalm and learning to put what you are reading into your own words. That is where Day Three comes in. I have provided space for you to write your own psalm or to rewrite the psalm of David in your own words.

The psalms of David are nothing more than journals containing his thoughts about God and his honest reactions to the affairs of life. You will notice that David is extremely blunt and unafraid to share what he is thinking. But he is also respectful of God, always showing Him the reverence He is due. There is a sense in which we are afraid to openly share our thoughts with God. We somehow believe that if we share what we are really thinking, we will shock God. But as you will find out from studying these psalms, there is nothing that God does not already know, including your unspoken thoughts. God can handle our frankness. He is not surprised when we share how we feel, or turned off by our anger, frustration, questions or doubts. But David is going to help us understand that our God is greater than our doubts. He is bigger than any feelings of frustrations we may experience or bouts of confusion we may face.

It is my hope that you will learn the joy that comes to being honest with God and the peace that comes when you discover that you can trust Him. Don't be in a rush. The goal is not to get done with this book, but to grow closer to God and better equipped to understand His character and more comfortable with your own need for Him in your life.

PSALM 3 – DAY 1

The Lifter of My Head.

But you, O Lord, are a shield around me; you are my glory, the one who holds my head high. – Psalm 3:3 NLT

David has had to abandon Jerusalem and his throne because his own son, Absalom, has taken over his kingdom. You can read about this tragic event in David's life in 2 Samuel 15. Psalm 3 was written at the time that all this was going on. So David was going through some significantly trying circumstances. He had lost everything, including his kingdom and the love of his own son. Everyone has seemingly turned against him. His enemies are taunting him that God will never rescue him from this predicament. But David knew something about his God. He had a confidence in God that came from experience. He knew that his God was a shield about him – a form of protection from attack. No matter how bad things got, David knew God to be as reliable as a shield a soldier used in battle to protect himself from certain death. David also knew that God was his glory – He was the one who gave David honor in the sight of others. David may have lost his throne, but he knew he was in God's hands. Others may have lost their respect for David, but he knew that ultimately any honor he received was from God and not from his position or possessions. It was God who gave David's life "weight," as the word glory can be translated. In other words, it was David's relationship with God that gave his life value – not his job, title, or resume. Finally, David knew that it was God who held his head high. It would have been easy for David to hang his head in defeat under the circumstances. He was running away from his own son. He had abandoned his own throne and was hiding in the wilderness. But David knew that God was the lifter of heads. He would revive David and ultimately restore Him to his throne – if that was God's desire. As he left the city that day, David was able to say, "If the Lord sees fit, he will bring me back to see the Ark and the Tabernacle again. But if he is through with me, then let him do what seems best to him" (2 Samuel 15:25 NLT).

3

David knew his God. He had faith in his God. He could rest in his God. He had confidence in his God. So he cried out to his God. And then he waited. David was not going to let circumstances determine His view of God. A bad day was not going to alter his understanding of the goodness of God. Unexpected, unwelcome events should not cause us to doubt God, but should cause us to turn to Him for help, hope, and healing. Cry out. He answers.

Father, give me the confidence of David. Give me a view of you that is not determined by my circumstances. Help me to see Your faithfulness in the midst of difficulty. Help me to trust You even when things seem out of control, unfair, difficult to understand. You are my shield, glory, and the lifter of my head. Amen

PSALM 3 – DAY 2

Lord, sometimes I just don't understand you;
I have a hard time seeing what you are doing.
My circumstances scream out, "He is not there!"
They tease me, "Your God does not care!"

But Your Word paints a different picture.
It reveals that You are in control and in love with me.
You watch over me, protect and provide for me.
You know my circumstances better than I do.
And You have a plan to perfect me through them.

I can choose to worry,
or I can choose to rest.
I can spend all my time staring at what is going on around me,
or I can fix my eyes on You.

Help me to see You in the midst of my circumstances,
but also in spite of them.
Teach me to trust You,
even when I don't fully understand You.
Don't let me judge Your goodness
by what I consider to be a bad situation.

Reveal Your strength through my weakness;
Your knowledge through my ignorance.
Open my eyes so that I can see You,
even if my circumstances never change.

PSALM 3 – DAY 3

Write Psalm 3 in your own words or write a psalm of your own. Be honest and open. Don't be afraid to tell God how you feel, but also include praise for who He is and all that He has done and is going to do in your life.

PSALM 4 – DAY 1

Set Apart By God, For God.

You can be sure of this: The Lord set apart the godly for himself. The Lord will answer when I call to him. – Psalm 4:3 NLT

More than likely this Psalm was written shortly after Psalm 3. David has had to abandon Jerusalem because his son, Absalom, has taken over his kingdom. David is in hiding somewhere in the wilderness outside Jerusalem. His own son has been spreading lies about him, ruining his reputation and turning the hearts of the people against him (2 Samuel 15:1-5). These are difficult days for David. He is facing one of the toughest moments of his life, having to listen to false accusations against himself, and watching as his kingdom is taken over by his own son. The natural response would have been anger. But instead, David turns to God. In spite of the circumstances, David knew that his God was still for him. He reminds himself and us, "You can be sure of this: The Lord set apart the godly for himself. The Lord will answer when I call to him" (Psalm 4:3 NLT). The Hebrew word translated "set apart" is *palah* and it means "to be distinct, separate, set apart, to be different."[1] It conveys the idea of God distinguishing one thing from another. David knew that God was going to deal with him differently because he belonged to God. David refers to himself as "godly." That word simply means "faithful one." David is saying that he has been faithful to God. He is not claiming perfection or sinlessness, but only that he has not abandoned God. He continued to trust in God. He belonged to God, so he knew that God would hear him when he called.

The people who accompanied David when he fled Jerusalem were asking him, "Who will show us better times?" (Psalm 4:6 NLT). They were distraught and wondering what was going to happen to change their circumstances. They wanted to know when things were going to get better.

---

[1] Warren Baker, Eugene Carpenter, *The Complete Word Study Dictionary Old Testament* (Chattanooga, TN, AMG Publishers, 2003), 901

David knew that God was the key to their hope. He knew from experience that God was the source of joy. God had given David more joy than any amount of success or affluence could ever bring. "You have given me greater joy than those who have abundant harvests of grain and new wine" (Psalm 4:7 NLT). David knew that God alone could hear him when he called, declare him to be innocent, free him from all his troubles, show him mercy, and keep him safe even in his sleep. No matter what was going on around him and to him, David knew that he could trust God.

Father, I want to trust You more. I want to have the confidence in You that David expressed. He had found You to be faithful in the past, so he could confidently trust You for the future. He did not let the conditions around him determine His faith in You. He trusted in Your character, not his circumstances. He recalled all the wonderful things You had done for him and realized that You had set him apart for Yourself. David belonged to You, so he knew he could trust You. That is how I long to see You. Amen

PSALM 4 – DAY 2

These are difficult days, Lord,
A good friend has died and it all seems so unfair.
It feels as if Satan is laughing,
And our side has lost another valuable player!

It's hard to understand how this could be part of Your plan.
It seems unjust and unfair.
It makes no sense. It seems unproductive.
There has to be a better way than this!

But I know You know what You are doing.
I trust You because You are trustworthy.
You have never given me reason to doubt You,
So why should I start now?

I suffer from a limited perspective.
I can only see so far and then everything becomes blurry.
But You know all things and see all things,
The future is as clear to You as the past.

Nothing surprises You or catches You off guard.
At no time are You in heaven wringing Your hands in worry.
You are in complete control,
Which should bring me complete peace.

Give me eyes to see life from Your perspective.
Replace my limited perspective with an eternal one.
Let me see You when everyone else around me sees nothing.
But when I can't see You, help me trust You anyway.

I know You are God. I know You love me.
I know You are all-powerful and in complete control.
But help me believe those things
When everything around me shouts otherwise.

I put my hope and trust in You.
I give You my confusion and my questions.
Show me mercy. Shower me with grace.
Shine in the darkness and light my way, O Lord!

PSALM 4 – DAY 3

Write Psalm 4 in your own words or write a psalm of your own. Be honest and open. Don't be afraid to tell God how you feel, but also include praise for who He is and all that He has done and is going to do in your life.

PSALM 5 – DAY 1

A Knowledge of God.

But let all who take refuge in you rejoice; let them sing joyful praises forever. Spread your protection over them, that all who love your name may be filled with joy. For you bless the godly, O Lord; you surround them with your shield of love. – Psalm 5:11-12 NLT

Where does David go in times of trouble? He goes to God. He turns to the only one who can help him. He cries to God for help – as his King and Lord – and then he waits expectantly. As a king himself, David understood the sovereign rule of God. He was in charge. He alone possessed the power and authority to do anything about David's problem. But he was also David's God, so He deserved honor, respect, and worship. David understood the holiness and righteousness of God, that He was set apart and separate from the sinfulness of men – including the wicked, prideful, evil doers, liars, murderers and the deceitful. God was not like earthly kings who could be all those things and more. He was a righteous, holy King – who was just, good, and merciful. So David could appeal to His unfailing love and ask for God to lead him in the right way to go. Unlike David's enemies, who lied and flattered for their own benefit, God was truthful, loving, and a righteous judge who always dealt justly and honestly with men.

David saw God as a place of refuge and protection. He could run to God in the tough times and find comfort in God's open, loving arms. Because David understood the mercy and love of God, he could sing praises even in the midst of suffering. He could experience joy even when surrounded by those who were out to destroy him. David had found God to be his protector and provider time and time again. God had proven Himself faithful to David in the past, so he knew he could trust him for the future. He knew if he called, God would hear. He knew if he was under attack, verbally or physically, God would protect him. He knew if his enemies attacked him unfairly, God would deal with them justly. He knew that when he was at a loss for what to do next, God would show him what to do. David knew God as his King, guide, protector, provider, judge, advocate, refuge, and holy God. God was his source of joy and peace, the object of his praise, the focus of his prayers, the answer to his problems, the director of his paths, and the reason for his worship. Oh, that I would know God like that. "Oh, that we might know the Lord! Let us press on to know him. He will respond to us as surely as the arrival of dawn or the coming of rains in early spring" (Hosea 6:3 NLT).

Father, I want to know You more. I want to have an understanding of Your character and nature like David did. Knowing You didn't rid David of all his problems, but it gave him a different perspective on how to handle and view them. I want to respond to the circumstances of life as he did – prayerfully, expectantly, worshipfully, and joyfully. I want to understand Your holiness better, rest in Your love more often, and sing Your praises in the good times and the bad times. Amen

PSALM 5 – DAY 2

A Healthy View of God.
Based on Psalm 5

I feel like I pray, but no one's there.
Even my groans go unnoticed.
You are my King, the ruler of my life,
And my God, the one who gave me life,
So ultimately, I'm calling out to You,
Expecting You to do something, because no one else can.

I know this about You, Lord: You aren't attracted to evil in the least,
You can't even stand having it around,
Including people who think more highly of themselves than they do of You.
You hate the behavior produced from a life lived in opposition to You.

Eventually, because You are God,
You will be forced to punish all who love falsehood more than truth,
Who take away life with their hands, or destroy reputations with their words.
You are holy and can't help but hate what is unholy.

But You are also loving – unceasingly so,
And it's because of Your love that I can even enter into Your presence.
So when I do, I come before You with an attitude of worship and awe.
I ask You to lead me and guide me and to protect me from my enemies.

There is no shortage of people out there who lie
And who desire to hurt others, including me.
They act as if they love me, flattering me with their words,
But they don't mean what they say.
But I will let You be their judge and not me.
You judge righteously, so give them whatever they deserve.
At the end of the day, their sin is against You, not me.
I'll leave them in Your hands.

But for all of us who love You and turn to You for help,
May we find refuge and, as a result, rejoice accordingly.
Help us understand more than ever just who You are — Your nature,
And discover the joy of trusting in You.
It's our relationship with You that makes us godly, not us,
So bless us and surround us with Your protection like a shield.

PSALM 5 – DAY 3

Write Psalm 5 in your own words or write a psalm of your own. Be honest and open. Don't be afraid to tell God how you feel, but also include praise for who He is and all that He has done and is going to do in your life.

PSALM 6 – DAY 1

God's Unfailing Love.

Return, O Lord, and rescue me. Save me because of your unfailing love. – Psalm 6:4 NLT

God rescues.
God saves.
God heals.
God shows compassion.
God hears.
God restores.
God answers.
God rebukes.
God disciplines.
God loves.

Those are just a few of the things that David knew about God. So when things weren't going so well in David's life, he turned to God. David was suffering greatly. We don't know why. He was weak, in agony, sick at heart, experiencing grief, and physically worn out from crying. He wasn't even sure if what he was going through was because of something he had done. It didn't seem to matter. Whether his suffering was the result of his own sin or the sin of someone else, he was going to turn to God. He was going to appeal to God's unfailing love and mercy. David says, "I am weak." His appeal is not based on his worthiness, but his weakness. He knew that he needed God. His strength was gone, his resources spent, his options eliminated. Like David, we need to come to the place where we understand our greatest argument before God is our NEED for Him. As long as we harbor any thoughts of self-sufficiency, we will miss out on God's unfailing love. It is not that He stops loving us, but that we fail to experience the full affects of that love because we keep trying to meet our own needs. James 4:6 reminds us that "God opposes the proud but gives grace to the humble." He opposes the prideful – those who resist Him and refuse to humble themselves before Him. But He shows favor to the humble – those who have been humiliated by circumstances or who simply understand their need for God and humbly come to Him for help.

David had a strong belief in God's ability to hear him and to do something about his situation. In fact, in verses 8-9 David speaks in the past tense. He says, "The Lord HAS heard my weeping. The Lord HAS heard my plea." Then he speaks confidently about the future: "The Lord WILL answer my prayer." David had confidence in his God. He understood His character. For David it was not a matter of *whether* God would act, but *when* He would. "How long, O Lord, until you restore me?" (Psalm 6:4 NLT). Isn't that the question we all ask? But only God knows the answer and He is not obligated to give us the answer. Joseph spent more than three years in a prison suffering for a crime he did not commit. The Israelites spent 70 years in captivity for sins they DID commit. God will act when the time is right. He will do what is needed right when it needs to be done. So we are to look to God, not for the solution to our problem. God may delay, but that does not mean God is not doing anything. Waiting is part of the process of trusting. It is while waiting for the answer that we learn to know the One from whom the answer will eventually come. The objective is NOT a solved problem, but the problem solver. We must seek to know God in the midst of our circumstances.

Andrew Murray puts it this way: "Waiting in the sunshine of His love is what will ripen the soul for His blessing. Waiting under the cloud of trial, that breaks in showers of blessing, is just as necessary. Be assured that if God waits longer than you could wish, it is only to make the blessing doubly precious. God waited four thousand years, until the fullness of time, before He sent His Son. Our times are in His hands, He will avenge His select speedily. He will make haste for our help and not delay one hour too long."[2]

Father, help me to learn to wait well. And while I am waiting, show me how to look for You. Don't let me obsess with the answer I am looking for, but instead, let me find my hope and satisfaction in You. Amen

---

[2] Andrew Murray, *Waiting On God* (Renaissance Classics, 2012), 60

PSALM 6 – DAY 2

God Is On My Side.
Based on Psalm 6

Lord, You are holy,
And have every right to be angry when I sin.
I know there are times when I deserve Your discipline,
When You are perfectly just in correcting me.
But I ask that you do it in compassion and not anger.
Discipline me, but do it in love.

I come to you in weakness, not worthiness,
Every ounce of my being needs your healing.
Even my heart is suffering and in pain.
I know You're going to do something, but when?

Return Lord, because it feels like You've left me.
I know You love me, so I ask that You rescue me – soon.
While death might seem like a relief,
I prefer to praise you on this side of the grave.

My circumstances have me worn out from sorrow,
I spend most nights crying instead of sleeping.
My eyes are constantly blurred with tears
Thanks to the events of life and the unsympathetic enemies in my life.

But here's what I know: You are completely aware of my situation.
You have heard my crying, seen my tears;
And You are going to answer my call for help.
So all those who wish to do me harm better watch out.
God is just and He is going to give you what you deserve.
I may look defenseless, but I have God on my side!

PSALM 6 – DAY 3

Write Psalm 6 in your own words or write a psalm of your own. Be honest and open. Don't be afraid to tell God how you feel, but also include praise for who He is and all that He has done and is going to do in your life.

PSALM 7 – DAY 1

God Is Just.

I will thank the Lord because he is just; I will sing praise to the name of the Lord Most High. – Psalm 7:17 NLT

David has been falsely accused. He has been slandered by those who hate him and his former boss, King Saul, has been led to believe that David is out to kill him. But nothing could have been further from the truth. In spite of the fact that David had been anointed by God as Saul's eventual replacement as king of Israel, and that Saul had hired a team of 3,000 trained mercenaries to kill him, David had chosen to not seek revenge or attempt to expedite the end of Saul's reign. And he was suffering for it. So he called out to his God. He appealed to the one who was capable of doing something about his situation. And all David wanted was justice. He wanted God, as judge, to rule on his behalf. If he was guilty, he was willing to suffer the consequences. "O Lord my God, if I have done wrong or am guilty of injustice, if I have betrayed a friend or plundered my enemy without cause, then let my enemies capture me. Let them trample me into the ground and drag my honor in the dust" (Psalm 7:3-5 NLT).

But David was confident in his innocence. He knew that God was all-knowing and well aware of what was going on inside his heart. "For you look deep within the mind and heart, O righteous God" (Psalm 7:9b NLT). So he begs God, "Declare me righteous, O Lord, for I am innocent, O Most High!" (Psalm 7:8b NLT). David had a strong grasp of God's role as judge of all mankind. He also knew that God was a righteous judge. He ruled rightly in all cases. He had no trouble believing that God was fully capable of bringing down the hammer on those who were guilty and unrepentant. "If a person does not repent, God will sharpen his sword; he will bend and string his bow. He will prepare his deadly weapons and shoot his flaming arrows" (Psalm 7:12-13 NLT). God was not only capable of judging rightly and justly, but of bringing the appropriate punishment when guilt was established.

David had no confidence in the justice and fairness of men. He knew men well. He had been burned by them before. David was well aware of the deceitfulness of the human heart. He wrote about it often. "The wicked are stringing their bows and fitting their arrows on the bowstrings. They shoot from the shadows at those whose hearts are right" (Psalm 11:2 NLT). "Don't let me suffer the fate of sinners. Don't condemn me along with murderers. Their hands are dirty with evil schemes, and they constantly take bribes" (Psalm 26:9-10 NLT). David put his trust and confidence in the justice of God. He knew he could trust God to judge fairly, impartially, righteously and accurately. He knew God would defend him, protect him, and ultimately save him – because he was innocent. So David declared, "I will thank the Lord because he is just; I will sing praise to the Lord Most High" (Psalm 7:17 NLT). David expresses gratitude and offers praise to the sovereign ruler over all the universe who vindicates the innocent and judges the wicked. He knew God to be just. He knew God to be an honest judge who is always right and never wrong. He knew God was fully aware of all the facts and would never accuse wrongly or punish undeservedly. The wicked would receive what they deserved. The innocent – those whose hearts are true and right – would receive justice. Because God is just.

Father, You are just and right in all You do. You never punish inappropriately or decide a case wrongly. You are the honest judge. You are the righteous judge. You are the holy judge. I can trust You. Amen

PSALM 7 – DAY 2

God, My Righteous Judge.
Based on Psalm 7

I come to You, O God, for any hope of protection,
Fully expecting You to defend me from those who harass me.
If You don't, I am in deep trouble.
They'll rip me to pieces like a lion would a lamb,
Leaving me a bloody mess with no hope of rescue.

You are my God, You know me.
If I have done anything wrong to deserve this,
If I am guilty of injustice in either word or deed,
If I have done anything to hurt a friend
Or unknowingly helped his enemy,
Then let those who are after me catch me.
Let them do whatever they want to me,
And leave me dishonored and humiliated.

But here's what I ask of You as my God:
Rise up in my defense! Stand up for me!
Let Your righteous anger bring a just ruling on my enemies!
Bring everybody into Your court of Law,
Show them who is boss, that You are the one who rules.
You alone have the right to judge the world and all who are in it.

As my judge, I ask that You decide my case, because I am NOT guilty!
I long for the day when the wicked get what they deserve,
And the righteous are honored by You.
Because You are God, You know the difference between the two.
You examine the hearts of men and know their true motives.

You are my God, my protector,
You are a Savior to all those whose hearts are Yours.

You are a judge who makes right decisions,
Speaking out against injustice every single day.

If a person refuses to turn to You and keeps on sinning,
You will be forced to give them what they deserve.
Your righteous justice will come like an enemy in battle,
You will use every weapon at Your disposal to dispose of them.

These people are like a woman suffering labor pains,
Their actions have left them pregnant,
And eventually they will bring into the world more lies, deceit and wickedness.
These people are always looking for ways to harm others,
But only end up hurting themselves in the end.
All the grief they intended for others ends up in their own laps.
They don't realize just how self-destructive their lifestyle really is.

And all this makes me grateful to God for His justice.
It makes me want to sing His praises,
Because He is in full control and will make all things right!

PSALM 7 – DAY 3

Write Psalm 7 in your own words or write a psalm of your own. Be honest and open. Don't be afraid to tell God how you feel, but also include praise for who He is and all that He has done and is going to do in your life.

PSALM 8 – DAY 1

The Greatness of God.

O Lord, our Lord, your majestic name fills the earth! Your glory is higher than the heavens. – Psalm 8:1 NLT

Immensity, power, glory, might, greatness. All those concepts are wrapped up in the single word translated "majestic" in this passage. And David uses it to describe the *name* of God, which speaks of His reputation or fame. To David, the greatness of God was everywhere. It was visible and tangible, but you had to be able to recognize it all around you. David saw it on the earth and in the night sky. God's glory – His reputation, renown and fame – was all-pervasive to David. He couldn't look out the window and not see the majesty of God revealed. He couldn't gaze into the night sky and not be reminded of the greatness of God. To David, God's reputation was not only based on His miraculous interventions in the affairs of Israel – His victories in battle, His divine provision and protection – but it was evident in the everyday affairs of life. Everything around David screamed the praise of God, because that is the way God designed it. Even Jesus understood what David was talking about when He quoted this Psalm in an exchange with the religious leaders.

> *The leading priests and the teachers of religious law saw these wonderful miracles and heard even the children in the Temple shouting, "Praise God for the Son of David." But the leaders were indignant. They asked Jesus, "Do you hear what these children are saying?"*
>
> *"Yes," Jesus replied. "Haven't you ever read the Scriptures? For they say, 'You have taught children and infants to give you praise.'"* – Matthew 21:15-16 NLT

From birth, man was made to praise God. We are appointed for that purpose. But the effects of the fall and the influence of sin have a way of hijacking our purpose and blinding us to the majesty and greatness of God.

We lose the ability to see Him all around us. Our eyes become blind to His presence and power.

When Jesus entered Jerusalem just days before His crucifixion, the crowd of disciples following Him cheered wildly, proclaiming, "Blessings on the King who comes in the name of the Lord! Peace in heaven, and glory in highest heaven!" (Luke 19:38 NLT). The Pharisees were appalled at what they heard and demanded that Jesus tell His disciples to cease and desist. Instead, Jesus replied, "If they kept quiet, the stones along the road would burst into cheers!" (Luke 19:40 NLT). Jesus knew what David knew. Everything in creation shouts the praise and glory of God. It all points back to our great, Creator God. While all men were created to praise God, many do not. But creation does. God's glory is not relegated to man's recognition of it. God's glory or reputation is evident everywhere and at all times.

And the amazing thing to David was that this glorious, majestic, mighty, all-powerful God would give any thought to men. We are insignificant when compared to creation. Yet God has not only taken note of us, He has given us a job to do. He has appointed us as stewards of His creation. He has given us responsibility over all that He has made and that gives us glory and honor. We get to care for what He has created. What an honor. What a privilege. The recognition of that vital role given to us by a mighty God should rock our world and cause us to exclaim with David, "O Lord, our Lord, your majestic name fills the earth!" We should recognize the greatness of God's reputation and want to do everything in our power to protect it, proclaim it, and live up to it.

Father, give me eyes to see You all around me. Don't let me look past Your divine presence in creation as I search for You elsewhere. Like David, may I be able to look out the window or up into the sky and see You. Let me be blown away by Your majesty, might, and glory. Amen

PSALM 8 – DAY 2

Our Great God.
Based on Psalm 8

You are Jehovah, OUR Master!
And Your greatness is visible everywhere –
Whether I look out the window or up into the night sky.
Even the cries of a baby and the babblings of a child speak of Your power,
Leaving those who oppose You speechless and powerless before You.
When I stare up into space I see just a portion of all You have made,
Only that which is visible to the naked eye.
And I can't help but ask the question:
Why would a God so great waste His time thinking about men,
Or even take a second to consider them at all?
But then it hits me – when You created Adam and Eve
You created them in Your own image
And surrounded them with the abundance and splendor of Your creation.
Then You put them in charge of it all!
Every sheep and cow, domestic or wild,
Birds of all kinds and even the fish that swim in the lakes and oceans.

You are Jehovah, OUR Master!
And Your greatness is visible everywhere!

PSALM 8 – DAY 3

Write Psalm 8 in your own words or write a psalm of your own. Be honest and open. Don't be afraid to tell God how you feel, but also include praise for who He is and all that He has done and is going to do in your life.

PSALM 9 – DAY 1

The Reputation of God.

Those who know your name trust in you, for you, O Lord, do not abandon those who search for you. – Psalm 9:10 NLT

David knew God. He was highly familiar with His character. He knew and understood His nature. The Psalms are more than a personal journal of David's experiences, they are an expression of his grasp of the greatness of God. In this Psalm alone, David reveals that his God is all-powerful, just, eternal, righteous, faithful, merciful, sovereign, impartial, holy, and wrathful. It was David's understanding of the nature of God that made it possible for him to trust God. To know God's name means "to be his follower, recognizing his authority and maintaining loyalty to him."[3] The word translated "name" can also mean "reputation or fame." To trust in the name of God was to trust in who He was – His very nature, character, and reputation. It was to stand on His past accomplishments and to rely on His track record of reliability. God had proven Himself to David time and time again. He had shown Himself to be faithful, powerful, righteous, just, true, merciful and holy. So David trusted in the name of God. When in trouble, he appealed to the name of God.

For David, God was worthy of praise because of all He had done in the past. He had found God to be a shelter and a refuge in the past, so he knew God would be so in the future. God was faithful, consistent, reliable and unchanging in His nature. David knew he could turn to God and find mercy and help no matter how difficult the situation. He knew from experience that God had a special affinity for the helpless and the hopeless, rescuing and restoring them. David had seen God judge righteously and justly, bringing judgment on the wicked and avenging the righteous. For David, the works of God were "unforgettable" and "marvelous." They

---

[3] *The NET Bible (New English Translation)*, (Biblical Studies Press, L.L.C., 2016)

were worth singing about, talking about, and relying upon. No matter how bad things got, David knew he could trust in his God, because he knew Him well.

Father, I want to know You like David did. I want to trust You like David did. I want to understand the full scope of Your character and be able to rest in the integrity of who You are based on all You have done. Give me eyes to see Your reputation all around me. Help me know You better and better with each passing day. Amen

PSALM 9 – DAY 2

In God We Trust.
Based on Psalm 9

From the depths of my heart I'm going to praise You,
And then I'm going to tell everyone all the great things You have done.
Because of You I have an over-abundance of joy,
And it comes out as songs of praise for Your remarkable reputation.

You caused my enemies to turn and run;
They went weak in the knees and dropped like dead men at the sight of You.
When it came time to pass judgment, You ruled in my favor.
As a righteous judge, You ruled fairly and justly.
The case against the nations has already been decided,
And their names have been stricken from the books.
Those who oppose You are done, without any hope,
And even their cities are long forgotten as far as You are concerned.

But while your enemies fade away, You reign forever,
And from Your throne You sit prepared to judge the world,
Justly, fairly and always rightly.
You rule on behalf of the oppressed,
Providing protection and a safe place to hide from their enemies.
But those of us who know Your character trust You,
because You have been proven faithful, never turning Your back on those who need You.

All of us should sing God's praises because He rules here on earth.
We should tell the world about all He has done for us.
There's no doubt that God gives murderers what they deserve,
But He also gives the helpless and the hopeless what they need most.
He doesn't turn a deaf ear to the cries of those in trouble.

Which is why I ask You to show me mercy, Lord.
I know you see what is happening to me.

I am as close to death as I have ever been,
So I ask you to provide a way of escape so I can give You the credit,
And hold a party to celebrate Your salvation.

It's amazing, but those who reject You and hate those who serve You
Have ended up falling into the trap they set for someone else.
But it shouldn't surprise me, because You are known for doing what is right
And giving the wicked exactly what they deserve in the end.

Eventually, all who oppose You will end up dead.
Spiritual death is the end result for all who fail to give You the honor You deserve.
But You will never fail to give those in need what they require,
You will not let the poor and oppressed suffer indefinitely.

So here is what I am asking Lord: Act now!
Don't let a bunch of weak-kneed, arrogant humans stand up to You.
Judge them. Give them something to fear.
Remind them that they are just men and You are God.

PSALM 9 – DAY 3

Write Psalm 9 in your own words or write a psalm of your own. Be honest and open. Don't be afraid to tell God how you feel, but also include praise for who He is and all that He has done and is going to do in your life.

PSALMS 11-12 – DAY 1

God Sees. God Knows. God Acts.

But the Lord is in his holy Temple; the Lord still rules from heaven. He watches everyone closely, examining every person on earth. – Psalm 11:4 NLT

We are surrounded by uncertainty. There seems to be nothing and no one we can count on any more. Politicians fail us, corporate leaders deceive us, friends disappoint us, and it seems as if everywhere we look, someone is out to take advantage of us. But David knew he could trust God. Why? Because God was holy, righteous and just. David found comfort in the realization that God was still in control, sitting on His throne in heaven where He saw all that was going on down here on earth. Yes, David felt the effects of living in a sinful world. He faced opposition, had his fair share of enemies, endured threats, suffered unfairly, and witnessed the attacks of the unjust against the just. From a human perspective, David felt like all was lost. He even asked, "What can the righteous do?" In the face of all that is going on around us and happening to us, what are those of us who love God supposed to do to make a difference?

David's answer? Trust God. Why? Because God is still on His throne. He is still in charge. He is wide awake and well aware of what is going on down here on earth. God sees – He perceives – He doesn't just look on in stunned shock, watching all the chaos taking place among men. He sees and He knows exactly what is happening, who is doing what to whom, and what needs to be done about it. His eyes are wide open and He sees into the hearts of ALL men, examining their motives and determining their fate. The Lord reminds us, "I have seen violence done to the helpless, and I have heard the groans of the poor. Now I will rise up to rescue them, as they have longed for me to do" (Psalm 12:5 NLT). God sees. God hears. God will act.

God is a just God who loves to do what is right. While everyone else is untrustworthy, undependable and unreliable, God is faithful, trustworthy and true. And He is powerful enough to back up His words with action. Not only is God aware of injustice, He is strong enough to do something about it. We have to believe that God is aware of our circumstances. Even when all hope appears lost, we must rest in the reality that God has not turned His back on us. He sees. He knows. He loves. He despises wickedness and honors righteousness. He loves to do what is right. Everything about Him hates injustice and evil. It may appear that He is indifferent when we look at all that is happening in the world, but we have to trust that one day God is going to set all things right. He may not do it in our time frame or even in our lifetime. We may not live to see it happen. But He WILL do what is right. Justice will be done. So we trust Him. We turn to Him. We wait for Him. God sees. God knows. And one day, He WILL act.

Father, some days I feel overwhelmed by all that is going on around me. Sometimes I feel as if it is just me against the world. I begin to lose hope and despair starts to set in. But today You reminded me that I can trust You. You know every detail of my life and are well aware of what is happening to me and around me. You see. And You are going to act. I can trust You. Amen

PSALMS 11-12 – DAY 2

God Is Still In Control.
Based On Psalm 11

When things get tough, everyone's advice seems to be to run and hide,
But I have learned to trust God for protection.
Those who oppose me are like soldiers preparing their weapons;
Getting ready to take pot shots at me in order to destroy me.
They especially seem to love attacking those who love God.
If we can't turn to God, our firm foundation,
In the midst of all this, what else are the righteous going to do?

But God is still there. He is still in His Holy Temple.
He still sits on His throne in heaven,
And nothing escapes His notice.
His eyes are wide open, examining the heart of every man,
Both the ungodly and the godly.
But He hates the actions of those who oppose Him and oppress others.
He will eventually bring down judgment on them
That is indescribably painful but totally justifiable.
I can rest in the fact that God is righteous and loves justice.
Those who stand as justified and innocent in His eyes
Don't need to fear seeing His face.

God Sees. God Knows. God Will Act.
Based On Psalm 12

Lord, we need Your help, because it seems like the godly are a vanishing breed,
Those who trust in You are few and far between.
Everyone lies to one another,
False flattery and deceptive words are all you hear anymore.
I wish You would just silence them all!
But they just boast and brag, taking great pride in their eloquence.
"We'll say whatever we want to say," they claim,
"And nobody can do anything about it!"

But God has something else to say about the matter.
He has seen how their lies and deception have hurt others,
And He isn't going to put up with it anymore.
God is going to rise up and provide deliverance
For those who are anxiously waiting for a Savior.

And we can take God at His word,
Because what He says, unlike what comes out of the mouths of men,
Is totally trustworthy, pure, and uncontaminated by lies.
So, Lord, we know You're going to come through.
You're going to protect the innocent,
And preserve the helpless.
Even though these people who love lies more than You
Seem to be as popular as they are populous.

PSALMS 11-12 – DAY 3

Write Psalm 11 in your own words or write a psalm of your own. Be honest and open. Don't be afraid to tell God how you feel, but also include praise for who He is and all that He has done and is going to do in your life.

PSALMS 11-12 – DAY 3

Write Psalm 12 in your own words or write a psalm of your own. Be honest and open. Don't be afraid to tell God how you feel, but also include praise for who He is and all that He has done and is going to do in your life.

PSALMS 13-14 – DAY 1

Because God Has, I Will.

But I trust in your unfailing love. I will rejoice because you have rescued me. – Psalm 13:5 NLT

What more does God have to do for you to get you to begin to trust Him? What is it going to take for you to really believe that He knows what is going on in your life and will provide for and protect you, regardless of what you see happening around you? That is the recurring theme of so many of the Psalms of David. It is clear that David was a man who had his fair share of trials and troubles. While he may have been a king and enjoyed great wealth and wielded tremendous power, he was not immune to problems. He faced a variety of difficult circumstances in his lifetime, including the constant threat of enemies, both within and without his kingdom. At one point, his own father-in-law, Saul, was on a crusade to have him killed. Later on in his life, David would watch as his own son, Absalom, led a rebellion against him and took over his kingdom. The Philistines never forgave him for killing their champion, Goliath. And there were times when David felt all alone and alienated from God. He was human and prone to look at his circumstances, questioning whether God was aware of what was happening to him. In the midst of his suffering and struggles, he would ask the same questions we all ask of God: "How long?" When is this going to stop, God? When will You step in and do something about this situation in my life? Why the delay? What are You doing? Why are You waiting?

Four times in the first two verses of Psalm 13, David repeats that question, "How long?" He pleads with God to answer him, to give him some glimmer of hope in the midst of the darkness. David wants to see God do something so his enemies won't gloat over his situation and mock he and God. But then David says the one thing we all need to be able to say: "But I trust in your unfailing love" (Psalm 13:5 NLT). Actually, the tense of the verb he uses speaks of a past event, a completed action. David is saying,

"But I have trusted in your unfailing love." David has continually lived his life by placing his confidence in the kindness and mercy of God. That's why he is able to say, "I **will** rejoice in your salvation." Because David had trusted in God in the past, he knew he could trust in God for the future. He knew that there was a day coming when God was going to bring salvation. He didn't know how or when, but he knew it was coming. He would rejoice one day. He would sing for joy one day. Why? Because God had been good to him in the **past**. The best way to translate verse 6 is "I **will** sing to the LORD, for he **has been** good to me." The basis for David's future joy was God's past provision. He knew that God **would** come through for him, because God **had** come through for him. David's God was a faithful, consistent and unchanging God. His God always delivered, always came through, never abandoned, never gave up, never walked out on him, and never disappointed.

From David's perspective, only a fool would reach the conclusion that there is no God (Psalm 14:1). Only a fool would decide that God was not there or did not care. David had seen the hand of God in the past and he knew he would see the hand of God in the future. Because God **had**, David knew he **would** sing, rejoice, and praise God some day – in spite of all that was going on at the moment.

Father, You have never failed to be faithful to me. So let me trust in Your past deliverance and there find hope for my future restoration. You are always faithful, always loving, and always powerful. Because You have, I can trust that you will. Your character is consistent and constant, never changing. Amen

PSALMS 13-14 – DAY 2

It's A Matter Of When, Not If.
Based on Psalm 13

Dear God, to be honest, sometimes it feels like You've forgotten me.
It seems like You've gotten busy someplace else or are distracted.
In the meantime, I end doing all kinds of self-examination,
To the point that even my soul suffers.
At times it even feels like unbelievers are better off than me.

All I ask is that You look at me and give me an answer, God!
I could use a little encouragement right now, because I'm dying here.
You don't want the "other side" to think they've won because I fell, do you?
The last thing you want is the enemy having a party at my expense.

But don't get me wrong. I have always believed that You love me;
And it's because You've saved me before, that I can rejoice even now.
I have confidence that a day is coming when I will be able to sing Your praises,
To rejoice in Your coming salvation, because You have always been good to me.

Know God Or No God.
Based on Psalm 14

Only an idiot what convince himself,
"There is no God."
But what else could he conclude,
When his life is characterized by sin, and he rarely does good?

But God has a perfect vantage point in heaven,
and is able to see every single human being.
He scans humanity for any sign of wisdom or insight,
To see if anybody really wants to worship and obey Him.
And His conclusion? Every single person has rebelled against Him.
As a race, they are morally filthy,
Nobody does what God wants them to do,
Not a single soul!

If they only knew the truth.
They are busy wolfing down the godly like bread,
When they should be calling out to God for mercy.
But the day is coming when those who said, "no God!,"
Will truly know God, but only in fear.
Because ultimately, God is on the side of the godly.
While you're busy trying to frustrate the plans of God's people,
God has made a promise to protect them.

It's my hope that the ultimate salvation of God will take place soon,
That He will put an end to all this and restore His people once and for all.
When He does, we will all rejoice. We will all sing with joy.

PSALMS 13-14 – DAY 3

Write Psalm 13 in your own words or write a psalm of your own. Be honest and open. Don't be afraid to tell God how you feel, but also include praise for who He is and all that He has done and is going to do in your life.

PSALMS 13-14 – DAY 3

Write Psalm 14 in your own words or write a psalm of your own. Be honest and open. Don't be afraid to tell God how you feel, but also include praise for who He is and all that He has done and is going to do in your life.

PSALMS 15-16 – DAY 1

How Unbelievable That God Is Accessible.

O my soul, you have said to the LORD, "You are my Lord, My goodness is nothing apart from You." – Psalm 16:2 NKJV

Who can be a welcome guest in God's house or become a permanent resident in the place where He lives?

Those are the questions that David uses to open Psalm 15, and they are a bit sobering and scary if you stop to think about them. What kind of person has the right to come into God's presence? What qualifies them to live their lives as God's neighbor, so to speak? David answers his own question by describing someone who lives a life of integrity. They are blameless. No, not perfect or without sin, but they attempt to live every area of their life out in the open – in front of God – with nothing hidden or compartmentalized. They are the kind of person whose actions are right and whose speech is marked by truth, not lies. They don't use words to hurt others or take advantage of them. They have a strong dislike for those whose lives are marked by a love for sin. But they recognize the value of those who love the Lord. They are promise keepers, not promise breakers. They share their money with others without demanding payment in return (plus a little something extra for their efforts). And they would never think of selling out someone just to pad their own wallet.

Wow! David says the person whose life is characterized by this kind of behavior is the one who will be left standing in the end. He or she will be welcome as God's guest and given a place in His presence. David covers virtually every aspect of an individual's life. Character, speech, conduct, values, integrity – even their finances. This is a person who shares God's heart. It's a portrait of someone whose life pleases God. But wait. How are we expected to pull this off? I don't always do what's right. I don't always speak the truth from a sincere heart. I sometimes gossip and I have been known to speak evil of my friends on occasion. There isn't one thing on

David's list of godly characteristics that I have managed to fulfill perfectly or completely. Which leads us right to Psalm 16. David knows the source of his integrity, honesty, right conduct, and pure motives. It's God. David appeals to God to keep him safe, to literally put a hedge of protection around him. He knows that it is only through God's help that any of us can come into His presence. He says, "You are my Lord, my goodness is nothing apart from You." In other words, only God can make a man good enough to qualify to come into His presence. God makes it possible for us to live the life David described in Psalm 15. Left to our own devices, we will sin and disqualify ourselves from ever entering God's presence. In Psalm 14, David said, "The Lord looks down from heaven on the entire human race; he looks to see if anyone is truly wise, if anyone seeks God. But no, all have turned away; all have become corrupt. No one does good, not a single one!" (Psalm 14:2-3 NLT). Paul takes up that same theme in his letter to the believers in Rome. "No one is righteous — not even one. No one is truly wise; no one is seeking God. All have turned away; all have become useless. No one does good, not a single one" (Romans 3:10-12 NLT). So what are we supposed to do? Paul goes on to tell us, "For no one can ever be made right with God by doing what the law commands. The law simply shows us how sinful we are. But now God has shown us a way to be made right with him without keeping the requirements of the law, as was promised in the writings of Moses and the prophets long ago. We are made right with God by placing our faith in Jesus Christ. And this is true for everyone who believes, no matter who we are" (Romans 3:20-22 NLT).

With David I say, "NO wonder my heart is glad, and I rejoice. My body rests in safety. For you will not leave my soul among the dead or allow your holy one to rot in the grave. You will show me the way of life, granting me the joy of your presence and the pleasures of living with you forever" (Psalm 16:9-11 NLT). God makes it all possible. From my ability to come into His presence right now to the assurance that I will one day live with Him forever.

Father, even my goodness comes from You. I can't live the life You've called me to live, so You sent Your Son to live it for me and die the death that I deserved for my sins. Now I can come into Your presence, not because of what I have done or deserve, but because of what Jesus did so that I might receive what I don't deserve: Your forgiveness, love and the assurance of eternal life. Amen

PSALMS 15-16 – DAY 2

The Bad News.
Based on Psalm 15

Who can be a welcome guest in Your house, God?
Or become a permanent resident in the place where You live?
Only the person whose life is completely, wholly Yours,
Nothing hidden, no secrets, no areas they try to keep from You.
It's the person who always does the right thing,
And never says the wrong thing.
They don't use their words to destroy reputations,
Bring discomfort, or attempt to get even.
They hate sin so much that they can't stand to be around sinners.
But they love being around those who love God.
They do what they are supposed to do – even when it costs them –
And share what they have with those in need,
Without expecting to profit from the exchange.
And they would never think of selling someone out
Just to pad their own wallet.
It's this kind of person who gets to stand before God.

The Good News.
Based on Psalm 16

I come to You for protection, God,
Fully expecting You to keep me from harm.
I call You, Adonia, my Sovereign Lord and Master.
It is You who makes possible any goodness in me.
Which is why those who are God's chosen make good friends,
And are truly worth associating with.
But as for those who choose to reject God,
They're only hurting themselves in the long run,
And I choose to have nothing to do with them.
I refuse to sacrifice my time, energy and talents to their sorry replacements for God.

God, You are all I have and all I need.
I am blessed right now because of You,
And my future is completely secure thanks to You.
You have made me Your child and all that is Yours is mine!

You guide and direct me, even in my sleep,
So why wouldn't I praise You?
You are always with me, right beside me,
Which gives me confidence to face any circumstance.

I am happy and secure, which results in joy.
I am at peace, physically, mentally and spiritually.
I know that when I die, I will not be separated from You.
I know that death is not the end, but just the beginning,
And even then You will be guiding my way,
Leading me right into Your very presence
Where I will get the pleasure of spending eternity with You.

PSALMS 15-16 – DAY 3

Write Psalm 15 in your own words or write a psalm of your own. Be honest and open. Don't be afraid to tell God how you feel, but also include praise for who He is and all that He has done and is going to do in your life.

PSALMS 15-16 – DAY 3

Write Psalm 16 in your own words or write a psalm of your own. Be honest and open. Don't be afraid to tell God how you feel, but also include praise for who He is and all that He has done and is going to do in your life.

PSALM 17 – DAY 1

The Ultimate Objective.

Because I am righteous, I will see you. When I awake, I will see you face to face and be satisfied. – Psalm 17:15 NLT

David is under extreme pressure. He is being hounded by King Saul, hunted down like a common criminal with a bounty on his head. Saul has hired 3,000 armed mercenaries to find David and kill him. So David finds himself hiding in the wilderness and running for his life. Talk about stress. Talk about anxiety. So David calls out to God. He pleads for God to act as his judge and find him innocent of any charges brought against him. He asks God to declare him innocent because he knows that he has done nothing to deserve this treatment from Saul. In verse three he reminds God that He has already tested him before. David uses terminology that indicates that his life has been anything but easy. He says "You have tested my thoughts." That word "tested" is a word used of refining metal. God has already put David in the furnace and proved the purity of his heart. He says that God has already "examined his heart" in the night. The reference to night is a poetic term that can also refer to a time of calamity or emotional darkness. In other words, David is saying that God has had the chance to observe David during the difficult days of his life. He has had plenty of opportunity to find fault in David. But David says that God has "scrutinized me" and found nothing wrong. Again, David uses terminology related to working with metal. He says that God has used trials to put him through the fire in order to purge any impurities from him. And as a result, David is innocent and sinless in regards to his relationship with Saul.

David appeals to God's mercy, grace, righteousness and love. He asks God to guard him, hide him and protect him. He begs God to come between he and his enemies, to bring them to their knees. In verse 14, David describes his enemies as wicked. Then in verse 15, he elaborates on just what these people are like. He says, "they look to this world for their reward." They are worldly, not godly. The are in love with this world and all that in can offer them. They don't see a future or believe in an afterlife or eternity, so they live as if this life is all there is. David looks around and sees these people enjoying prosperity, getting all that they desire, having lots of kids and leaving all their wealth to them. But at the end of the day, David puts his hope in what happens *after* life. He knows there is an eternity for all men. That the righteous God of the universe will one day judge all men and hold them accountable for their actions during this life. David rests content that God will declare him righteous and allow him to come into His presence. That is what brings David contentment even in the face of adversity. He knows that his ultimate satisfaction will come when He stands before God in heaven. This world is passing. This life is not all there is. The injustices and inequities of this life will one day be made right by God. That doesn't stop David from crying out to God for His help and deliverance here and now. But David knows that he can't judge the faithfulness and love of God solely based on how things go in this life. God is not done. As judge of the world, His final ruling has not yet been made. But David knows that even if his enemies catch him and kill him, he will stand before the Lord and find complete satisfaction for all life's trials, injustices and inequities.

Father, don't let me lose sight of eternity. Don't let the trials of this life rob me of the reality of eternal life. This is not all there is. There is more. When faced with difficulties, help me see them as You refining me, purifying me and removing from me the sin that still resides within me. You are constantly testing me, putting me through the heat of life, exposing and removing the impurities of my sin nature. Thank You for loving me enough to purify me. You are constantly making me more like Your Son and for that I am grateful. Amen

PSALM 17 – DAY 2

A Prayer of Ken.
Based on Psalm 17

O Lord, I am appealing my case to You, please listen.
I beg You to pay close attention to my calls for help.
Hear my prayer and answer,
Because I am telling You the truth!
All I ask is that the decision regarding my case come from You,
Because I trust that You are able to see what is really going on.

You have repeatedly proved the purity of my heart;
You've observed me during times of adversity and darkness.
When I was put through the fire of difficulty and refined by You,
It resulted in a lack of impurity and sin.
And I don't plan on saying anything I will regret now.
When it comes to what men do,
It is only by obeying the words from Your lips
That I have avoided living a life of violence and destruction.
There is no doubt that You have kept me on the right track,
Preventing me from losing my footing on my way.

God, I have full confidence that because I have called,
An answer is coming from You.
Please take a minute and listen to what I have to say.
Make Your love and mercy stand out.
Use Your power to save those who trust in You
And who come to You for protection when they are oppressed.
Watch over me like I was Your prized possession,
Put me under Your wing like a bird does its chick,
Because I am surrounded by those who are out to destroy my soul.
These people are imprisoned by their own prosperity,
They boast arrogantly.
They seem to be everywhere I go,

And they keep their eyes peeled like a half-starved lion looking for prey –
A young lion hiding in the shadows waiting to pounce.

Stand up and show Your power, Lord!
Disrupt this "cubs" plans, bring him to his knees.
Use Your sword to provide me with a way of escape.
Save me from men who love this world more than You,
Who seek all they need from this life instead of from You,
Who fail to recognize that their prosperity comes from You,
And that the affluence their kids enjoy, You provide.
But as for me, I know that my satisfaction comes from knowing You,
And even if all this ends in death, I will see You because You consider me righteous.

PSALM 17 – DAY 3

Write Psalm 17 in your own words or write a psalm of your own. Be honest and open. Don't be afraid to tell God how you feel, but also include praise for who He is and all that He has done and is going to do in your life.

PSALM 18 – DAY 1

Describing the Indescribable.

I love you, LORD; you are my strength. The LORD is my rock, my fortress, and my savior; my God is my rock, in whom I find protection. – Psalm 18:1-2 NLT

The imagery used in this Psalm is classic David. The simple, yet powerful words used by David to describe his God are found throughout the Psalms he penned. They are a vivid example of someone trying to describe the indescribable using terminology that is familiar to him and to which he can easily relate. David refers to God as his strength, rock, fortress, savior and a source of protection. It is because of these attributes that David loves the Lord. These words describe what God IS to David. They illustrate characteristics of God that have come to mean much to this "man after God's own heart". This Psalm was likely written late in David's life because it is almost a word-for-word copy of the song David sings near the end of his life that is recorded in 2 Samuel 22. David is near death and he is remembering all that God has done for him over a long, distinguished and sometimes difficult life. C. H. Spurgeon calls this Psalm "The Grateful Retrospect." David is expressing appreciation, praise, and love for God's unmistakable role in his life. He goes on to describe what God has done by using words like:

Pays back
Subdues
Rescues
Holds me safe
Saves me
Gives victory
Shows unfailing love

David opens up this Psalm with praise for God's characteristics. Then he closes it the same way. It is a classic chiastic structure, where the first half of the Psalm mirrors the second half. But the main point is found at the beginning and the end. God is David's rock – his *sela* in Hebrew – a rock, cliff, or a hollowed-out place in a rock that provides safety, refuge and protection. Why would David describe God in those terms? Why would a king who lived in the luxury of a palace use that kind of imagery? You have to remember that at one point, early in his life, David spent over ten years hiding in the wilderness, attempting to keep from being killed by King Saul. He hid in caves and lived in the remote wilderness, finding refuge and protection among the cliffs, rocks, and mountains.

This less-than-ideal environment had been David's home. It was where he hid from his enemy and found refuge in times of difficulty. Those rocks and caves became very familiar to David and they were a constant reminder of God's protection and love. They may have looked remote, foreboding and uninviting, but to David they were familiar and comfortable. There were probably many times during his reign when he would have preferred to be back in those same caves. In fact, when his son, Absalom, stole his kingdom from him, David headed back to the wilderness again. It was familiar territory where he knew God would meet him and provide for him.

Where do you and I run when times get tough? Do we have a place where God has showed Himself strong in the past? If we had to pick words to describe who God is to us and what He has done for us, which ones would we use? David spoke of God from experience. His knowledge of God and love for Him was not academic in nature, but from first-hand, real-life experience. I love what Eugene Peterson says about David and his relationship with God:

> The single most characteristic thing about David is God. David believed in God, thought about God, imagined God, addressed God, prayed to God. The largest part of David's existence wasn't David, but God. The evidence of David's pervasive, saturated awareness of God is in his profusion of metaphors: bedrock, castle, knight, crag, boulder, hideout. David was immersed in God. Every visibility revealed for him an invisibility.[4]

That is the kind of relationship I long to have with God. I want to be able to see Him all around me, to view Him through all my circumstances. The words we use to describe God are a great indicator of just how well we know Him.

---

[4] Eugene Peterson, "Leap Over A Wall" (San Francisco, Harper, 1997) 56

Father, You are my provider, banker, counselor, guide, shelter, the Kevlar vest I wear when the enemy attacks, the umbrella that keeps me dry in the storms of life, the life preserver when my boat goes down under me, the warm fire when the lights go out and the heat goes off, the unexpected check in the mail when my account was empty and my hopes were lost. Father, You have been there for me so often in my life. You have never failed to provide for me, protect me, and shower me with Your grace. Thank You! Amen

PSALM 18 – DAY 2

Old Faithful.
Based on Psalm 18

I love you, Lord, because You have proven Yourself strong over and over again.
You've been a place of refuge for me,
You've protected me, sheltered me, provided a way of escape for me.
You've been like a solid rock wall, a Kevlar vest, and a lethal weapon.
Every time I have turned to You, You've come through for me.

I could go on and on about the various ways You have rescued me.
When I felt like all was lost, and I had no more hope,
I knew I could call out to You. I could tell You my troubles,
And You would hear me, and then do something about it.
Sometimes Your response was immediate and earth-shattering.
You rocked my world and blew away my expectations,
Doing far more than I anticipated or even deserved.

But then there were other times when You seemed to delay,
Your response was late in coming, and sometimes not exactly what I wanted.
But You always answered. You always came through.
It was as if You reached down from heaven and personally handled my problem.
Sometimes You have had to rescue me.
Other times You've simply supported me or provided me with guidance.
On more than one occasion, You've had to protect me.
All along the way, I have tried to serve You and remain faithful to You.
But the real reason You reward me with Your love and mercy
Is because You have claimed me as Your own.
You are faithful to the faithful,
You are a God who acts with integrity to those who aspire to live with integrity.
You have a heart for the pure, the humble, the innocent.
In other words, You love those who love You and are being transformed by You.

KEN MILLER

Over the years, I have seen the truth of this lived out in my own life.
In the midst of all the instability of this world, You remain the solid rock.
You are unchanging in Your nature, consistent in Your character.
It is only because of You that I have the strength to live life,
The wisdom to make right decisions,
The endurance to walk the walk of faith,
And to stay on the path without wandering into the weeds.
Any success I have had is because of You.
Any victories I have enjoyed were Your doing, not mine.
My status as a child of God is because You adopted me in spite of me.

So for all of these reasons, I praise You.
You deserve it, I most certainly owe it, and so I gladly give it.
I can leave all my enemies in Your hands.
You will deal with them as You see fit.
The important thing is that You rescue me when I'm in trouble,
Protect me when I am helpless,
Shelter me when I am left out in the cold,
And save me when I can't save myself.
So I praise You even in the midst of a world that doesn't know You.
I express my love to You even when I am surrounded by those who hate You.

PSALM 18 – DAY 3

Write Psalm 18 in your own words or write a psalm of your own. Be honest and open. Don't be afraid to tell God how you feel, but also include praise for who He is and all that He has done and is going to do in your life.

PSALM 19 – DAY 1

The Power Of The Word Of God.

May the words of my mouth and the meditation of my heart be pleasing to you, O LORD, my rock and my redeemer. – Psalm 19:14 NLT

The power and glory of God is clearly evident in His creation. His greatness is mirrored in the vastness of the universe, the inexhaustible energy of the sun, and the countless stars in the sky. But when it comes to revealing Himself to man, God didn't stop there. David knew God through His Word. He discovered the greatness of God revealed in the Law of God. He had learned that God's Law revives the soul, gives the naive much-needed wisdom, brings joy to the heart, helps men see life more clearly, and on top of all that it warns and rewards. David found the words of God more desirable than gold and more appetizing than his favorite sweet. And as king of Israel, David had access to wealth and great food, so he knew what it meant to attempt to have his desires satisfied through materialism and hedonism. Money doesn't last, a great meal only leaves you hungry and desiring more. Nothing satisfies like the Word of God.

One of the things David learned about God's Word is its ability to see into his heart and reveal what's hidden there. It has the unique capacity, like an x-ray, to look into our soul and reveal sins – even those committed unknowingly or unintentionally – that we can't even see ourselves. But God's word not only reveals them, it can cleanse us from them. And it can protect us from committing sins out of presumption or sheer arrogance. David knew that his righteousness was dependent upon God's faithful, reliable, pure, trustworthy, totally correct, completely sound Word. It was only through time spent reading and meditation on God's Word that David's life could live a life that was pleasing to God. It is the Word of God and the indwelling presence of the Spirit of God that transforms our speech, our thoughts and our actions.

Father, Your Word is invaluable and irreplaceable. There is nothing else like it in the universe that can transform my life and bring joy, peace, wisdom, direction and satisfaction. Continue to increase my love for it, obedience to it, and dependence upon it. Let me love it like David did. Use Your Word to see into my heart and reveal what I can't see. Transform me by it. Equip me with it. Convict me through it. And never let me walk without it. Amen

PSALM 19 – DAY 2

The Glory Of God.
Based on Psalm 19

I look up at the sky and see the glory of God on display.
The night sky is like a canvas filled with His artwork.
The planets and stars can't speak, because they have no voice,
But You can hear what they are saying loud and clear.

The sun is right where it needs to be,
It bursts with light like a groom on the day of his wedding.
It tirelessly rises and sets, like a man with ceaseless strength.
Day after day, the sun does what God created it to do,
Providing heat and light to anything and everything.

But even greater than all that God has made is what He has said.
His written law, His principles for men to follow
Are perfect, complete, lacking in nothing.
His requirements for living life can be trusted,
And when the naive obey them, they gain wisdom.
His commands are always right,
And bring joy to the heart when they're kept.
His rules are completely without error or fault,
Providing insight to all those who follow them.
To fear God by keeping His commands is the right thing to do,
And we will be doing it for eternity.
Each judgment God has made is reliable,
And absolutely just.
They are to be valued more than money, even a lot of money.
They are more satisfying than honey,
Even the freshest honey straight from the honeycomb.
They teach those who keep them,
And they always come with consequences.

Without Your Word I wouldn't know what was in my own heart.
Use it to cleanse me from the sin hidden from my own view.
Let Your law prevent me from sinning presumptuously,
Don't let my own arrogance control me.
Then and only then will You see me as blameless,
And innocent of rebellion against You.

Let every word that I say and every thought that I have
Meet Your standards, O Lord,
Because You have been and always will be my Rock and Redeemer.

PSALM 19 – DAY 3

Write Psalm 19 in your own words or write a psalm of your own. Be honest and open. Don't be afraid to tell God how you feel, but also include praise for who He is and all that He has done and is going to do in your life.

PSALM 20 – DAY 1

In Times Of Trouble.

Some nations boast of their chariots and horses, but we boast in the name of the LORD *our God.* – Psalm 20:7 NLT

When your problems get solved and you've made it to the other side of your predicaments, to whom do you give the credit? Too often we end up giving ourselves a pat on the back for our ingenuity, determination and problem-solving skills. We unknowingly "boast" in our own power of self-preservation. We begin to believe that we can get ourselves out of any situation, given enough time, money, and patience. But David knew differently. He had learned from experience that when he encountered trouble, his first response should be to cry out to God. He knew that God was far more reliable and powerful – even though he was a king with all kinds of resources at his disposal. Whether it was a need for deliverance from an enemy or the fulfillment of a desire, David had learned to take everything to God. Nothing was too big or too small for God to handle. David knew that God answered prayer because He had done so in the past. God had delivered him before. God had saved, directed, and provided victory on more than one occasion, so David was more than willing to go back to the most reliable source he knew – God.

David's power was not determined by the size of his army, but by the object of his faith. As long as he turned to God and focused his faith on Him, David knew he had all the power he needed to face any difficulty, defeat any foe, and survive any situation. David says, "we boast in the name of the Lord our God." That word "boast" can be better translated "to recall, to think about, to make known."[5] David seems to be saying that, in times of trouble, we recall the character of God and lean on Him, not ourselves. We depend on His strength, not ours. We rely on His salvation instead of our own. Human strength is no match for God's power. Human

---

[5] Warren Baker, Eugene Carpenter, *The Complete Word Study Dictionary Old Testament* (Chattanooga, TN, AMG Publishers, 2003), 289

intelligence is a poor substitute for God's wisdom. Turning to God will always turn out better in the long run.

Father, You have a long track record of success and faithfulness. Yet we continue to turn elsewhere when times get tough. Continue to teach us to trust You alone, to turn to you first and to rely on You to the end. You will not disappoint. Amen

PSALM 20 – DAY 2

A Prayer Of Awareness.
Based on Psalm 20

It's my prayer that the next time you're in trouble
You cry to God so He can answer your call for help.
May the same God that kept Jacob safe keep you from harm.
I want you to discover just how holy and powerful He really is.
You'll find that He has seen all the sacrifices You have made,
And how you have been faithful in your attempts to worship Him.

It's my prayer that God give you the desires of your heart,
And help you succeed in all that you do.
Then we'll all have reason to rejoice with you
And to give God praise for what He has done for you.
We love it when God answers your prayers.

I have every confidence that God is going to save those He has chosen,
He is going to answer because He is holy and righteous.
He is going to rescue because He has the power to do so.
While other people might put their confidence in themselves,
As people of God, we trust in the reputation and character of God.
Self-confidence only results in disappointment and defeat,
But relying on God let's us stand firm no matter what comes our way.

PSALM 20 – DAY 3

Write Psalm 20 in your own words or write a psalm of your own. Be honest and open. Don't be afraid to tell God how you feel, but also include praise for who He is and all that He has done and is going to do in your life.

PSALM 21 – DAY 1

What's the Source Of Your Strength?

How the king rejoices in your strength, O LORD! He shouts with joy because you give him victory. – Psalm 21:1 NLT

In this Psalm, David, as the Lord's anointed king, recognizes that any victory or success he enjoys is attributable only to God and to God alone. David can't take any credit for any of it. He can't brag or boast about his own strength or his military capabilities. His army is not the source of his strength. His military prowess isn't either. It's God. He says, "the king rejoices in **your** strength, O LORD!" What a different perspective than that which pervades our society. We love to take credit for our victories and boast about our own capabilities. Even as Christians we can find ourselves puffing out our chests and basking in our own glory. But David reminds us that all glory belongs to God. David looks back over his life and recognizes the hand of God in all that he has accomplished as king. Sure, he went into battle, wielded his sword, suffered wounds at the hands of his enemies, killing his fair share of them, and came back tired and sometimes bloody. But he recognized the reality that God was the one who brought about the victory.

Over in the book of 2 Chronicles there is the story of the people of God facing tremendous odds against a far superior army. Jehoshaphat, the king of Judah, stood in front of the people and called out to God. He confessed their weakness and called on God to save them. He prayed, "you alone are the God who is in heaven. You are ruler of all the kingdoms of the earth. You are powerful and mighty; no one can stand against you!" (2 Chronicles 20:6 NLT). He went on to describe to God their dire circumstances and then called out, "O our God, won't you stop them? We are powerless against this mighty army that is about to attack us. We do not know what to do, but we are looking to you for help" (2 Chronicles 20:12 NLT). As they stood there waiting, the Spirit of God came upon an obscure man named Jahaziel. Under the inspiration of the Spirit of God, Jahaziel told the people, "This is what the LORD says: Do not be afraid! Don't be discouraged by this mighty army, **for the battle is not yours, but God's**" (2 Chronicles 20:15 NLT).

How did David know this same truth long before Jehoshaphat ever ascended to the throne of Judah? How could he be so certain that victory was God's doing, not man's? If you recall, long before David ever became king of Israel, he experienced first-hand the victory of God over a far superior enemy of his own. As a young man, he had come face to face with Goliath, a giant of a man who had ridiculed and taunted the men of Israel for days, challenging them to send out a champion to face him. He had no takers. That is until David showed up on the scene. And while every other Israelite soldier, including King Saul, cowered in the shadows, afraid to face their enemy in their own strength, David called out to him, "You come to me with sword, spear, and javelin, but I come to you in the name of the LORD of Heaven's Armies — the God of the armies of Israel, whom you have defied. **Today the LORD will conquer you**, and **I will kill you** and cut off your head. And then I will give the dead bodies of your men to the birds and wild animals, and the whole world will know that there is a God in Israel! And everyone assembled here will know that the LORD rescues his people, but not with sword and spear. **This is the LORD's battle**, and he will give you to us!" (1 Samuel 17:45-47 NLT). Notice what David said, "the Lord will conquer you, and I will kill you." Ultimately, he knew that this was going to be up to God. David had a role to play, but any success would be solely attributable to God. What a valuable lesson for us to learn today as we face the enemies in our lives. The battle is STILL the Lord's. Like David, we must learn to trust in the Lord and recognize that His unfailing love for us is what keeps us from stumbling in defeat. He is our champion. He is our strength. He is our victory.

Father, the battle has always been Yours. Forgive me for sometimes assuming that I bring something of value to the fight. I can do nothing without You. Victory is possible only through You. Continue to teach me to trust in You and to rest in the power You provide. Amen

PSALM 21 – DAY 2

Faith Is the Victory.
Based on Psalm 21

Even the guy you give the greatest strength knows to praise Your power, O Lord.
He recognizes that all his victories are Your doing, not his, and rejoices.
He has seen You answer his prayers, fulfilling his heart's desires.
You have blessed Him in so many ways, and given him authority and honor.
There was a time when he asked You to keep him alive,
And You blessed him with a long life and a lasting legacy.
He has lived long and well, and his impact will last forever.
What's amazing is You're the one who saves, and yet You allow him to receive honor.
You lift him up and allow him to share in Your glory.
But more than anything else, the blessings You give are eternal,
You assure him a place in Your presence forever.
How could he not trust in You?
Your love for him never fails and so his faith has a firm foundation.
Lord, it is You who will ultimately win all the battles,
You will use Your power to deal with all who oppose You.
There is a day coming when all men will be judged by You.
You will deal with them in Your righteous anger,
And give them exactly what they deserve.
The numbers of the wicked will finally stop growing,
As You deal with them once and for all.
They plot, scheme and devise all kinds of plans against You,
But they will never succeed.
In the end, they will run for their lives at the sight of You.
You deserve to be made much of, Lord, because of Your great strength.
So we will sing songs and boast about all the incredible things You have done.

PSALM 21 – DAY 3

Write Psalm 21 in your own words or write a psalm of your own. Be honest and open. Don't be afraid to tell God how you feel, but also include praise for who He is and all that He has done and is going to do in your life.

PSALM 22 – DAY 1

A Light In the Darkness.

His righteous acts will be told to those not yet born. They will hear about everything he has done. – Psalm 22:31 NLT

Moments of doubt and despair – we all have them – those days when everything seems to be going against us and even God appears nowhere to be found. Our prayers go unanswered and our hopes, unfulfilled. At those times, it is easy to fall into despondency and begin to view the world through lenses that have been darkened by doubt and clouded by the lies of the enemy. Even David, the man after God's own heart, was susceptible to having dark days of despair and Psalm 22 is a perfect illustration of how he handled those times in his life. He begins his Psalm by calling out to God. Notice his honesty and blatant frankness. He doesn't sugarcoat his feelings or attempt to put on a happy face for God. No, he asks God, "Where are you? Where have you gone? Why have you abandoned me?" David was not afraid to express his feelings to God. At that moment in his life he felt as if God had left him. He prayed, but received no answer. He cried out, but got no relief. But while David was honest with God, he was always respectful to God. He knew God was holy and deserving of his reverence and fear. He knew God to be trustworthy and faithful to rescue His people. So he knew that his feelings of abandonment, while real, were not a true picture of his God.

There is a huge difference between the reality of our circumstances and their ability to determine the reality and reliability of our God. Whatever was going on in David's life was difficult. He was surrounded by enemies and trouble. He was weak, worn out, lacking in strength, running out of hope, and fearing for his life. But he continued to call out to God. He knew that God was his strength and deliverer. The same God who had given him life at birth and protected him to this point, would protect him now. In spite of his circumstances, David knew he could count on God. He believed the time would come when he would be able to praise God for His deliverance. "For he has not ignored or belittled the suffering of the needy.

He has not turned his back on them, but has listened to their cries for help" (Psalm 22:24 NLT). David's trust in God was based on his understanding of God. He knew God well enough to know he could trust Him. He did not let his circumstances determine his faith.

Isn't it amazing that David, in his sorrow and despair, ended up writing a psalm that would reflect the very feelings of Jesus Himself as He hung on the cross. Psalm 22 is considered a Messianic psalm, prophesying the very suffering of the Lord Himself. Verses 11-18 paint a vivid picture of Jesus' last moments on the cross. "My life is poured out like water." "My tongue sticks to the roof of my mouth." "They have pierced my hands and feet." "They divide my garments among themselves and throw dice for my clothing." In the midst of his own suffering, David unknowingly echoed the future sufferings of Christ. Which should remind us that God the Father and Christ His Son understand fully what we are going through at any given moment. They understand our weakness and they know what it means to suffer. We are reminded of this in the book of Hebrews. "So then, since we have a great High Priest who has entered heaven, Jesus the Son of God, let us hold firmly to what we believe. This High Priest of ours **understands our weaknesses**, for he faced all of the same testings we do, yet he did not sin. So let us come boldly to the throne of our gracious God. There we will receive his mercy, and we will find grace **to help us when we need it most**" (Hebrews 4:14-16 NLT).

Father, You are not above my times of need and suffering. You are not distant and disinterested. You understand my weaknesses better than I understand them myself. You feel my pain. You empathize with my sorrow. You had to watch Your own Son suffer for my sins and die an agonizing death that was meant for me. And because He died, I can call out to You and receive mercy and grace when I need it the most! Thank You so much. Amen

PSALM 22 – DAY 2

Perception Versus Reality.
Based on Psalm 22

I'll be honest with you God.
Right now, it feels like you've left me,
Like You're nowhere to be found.
I call out to You, but You don't seem to hear me.
And if You do hear me, You don't answer.

But I know that You're holy,
And that people have been praising you for centuries.
You have a long history of rescuing Your people.
They cried out to You and you saved them.
They put their trust in You and You came through.

But I feel so undeserving.
I feel like I don't have a friend in the world.
Those who give me any attention at all,
Only mock me and ridicule what little faith I have, saying:
"Where's Your God now? Why isn't He saving you?"

But I can't help but remember that You gave me life,
You are the one that saw to it that I was born and lived.
From infancy, I have belonged to You.
You have always been my God.

So I call out to You and ask You to stay by me.
I am in trouble and there is no one else who can help.
I feel surrounded and overwhelmed.
It is as if everyone is out to destroy me, to rip me apart.
My strength is running low, my body aches,
My very heart is on the verge of giving up.
I feel like I have been out in the sun too long,

Like I am spiritually dehydrated and close to death.
My enemies seem to be everywhere,
They chase me like a pack of dogs, and I can't get away,
Because my hands and feet feel like they're nailed down.
I am emaciated and demoralized,
My enemies taunt me and ridicule me,
Divvying up all my possessions between them.

I beg you Father! Don't leave me!
You alone are my strength, and I need Your help.
Save me! Spare me!
Get me out of the mess I find myself in!

When You do, I will sing Your praises,
Everyone believer I know will hear me give You the glory.
We all need to praise You.
We all need to give You the honor and glory You deserve.
Because You have never ceased to rescue the helpless and hopeless.
You have never abandoned them or failed to answer their cries.

So I will lift up my voice and praise You in church,
I will make sure everyone I know hears what You have done.
I will tell them that You take care of the poor,
That all those who come to You will end up praising You,
Because You will give them ample reason to sing and rejoice.
One day the whole world is going to recognize You for who You are.
They will all eventually have to admit that You alone are God.
You are the all-powerful one.

Even those who aren't in need will end up worshiping You.
The poor to the wealthy, the youngest to the oldest
Will all bow down to You.
Even those who have yet to be born are going to hear about You.
Because we are going to have plenty of stories to tell
Of Your righteous acts and all that You have done.

PSALM 22 – DAY 3

Write Psalm 22 in your own words or write a psalm of your own. Be honest and open. Don't be afraid to tell God how you feel, but also include praise for who He is and all that He has done and is going to do in your life.

PSALM 23 – DAY 1

Only Sheep Appreciate A Shepherd.

The Lord is my shepherd. I have all that I need. – Psalm 12:1 NLT

What do you say about what is arguably the most well-known and popular psalm of all? The 23rd Psalm is probably the most familiar of all the psalms, for believers and non-believers. You can find it printed on plaques and coffee mugs, illustrated in paintings, and explained in countless books. It is short and simple, and yet the real message escapes most of us – because we don't live in an agrarian society. We don't know much about sheep or shepherds. So a lot of the imagery found in Psalm 23 escapes us. The relationship between a shepherd and his sheep seems rather pedestrian and simplistic to us. I mean, how hard could it be to care for sheep? They appear rather docile and far from demanding. But it's fascinating that God chose to use the metaphor of sheep on a regular basis when speaking of His people. In Matthew 10:6, Jesus referred to the Jews as the "lost sheep of the house of Israel." Reminiscent of Psalm 23, in the book of Ezekiel, God tells the people of Israel, " I myself will tend my sheep and give them a place to lie down in peace, says the Sovereign Lord. I will search for my lost ones who strayed away, and I will bring them safely home again. I will bandage the injured and strengthen the weak. But I will destroy those who are fat and powerful. I will feed them, yes—feed them justice!" (Ezekiel 34:15-16 NLT). Earlier in that same chapter, God refers to His people as sheep again, saying, "They have wandered through all the mountains and all the hills, across the face of the earth, yet no one has gone to search for them" (Ezekiel 34:6 NLT).

God saw His people as sheep. Jesus referred to Himself as the Good Shepherd. Why? What is the point behind this analogy of sheep and shepherds? The key to me is found in the words used in Psalm 23. David chooses his words carefully, and each carries significance. He speaks of need, rest, leading, renewal, guidance, fear, protection, and comfort. He paints a picture of total dependency as opposed to self-sufficiency. Sheep are not meant to defend for themselves. They are inherently dumb animals who wander easily and are prone to a herd mentality. Unlike deer, they do not readily sense impending danger. Unlike other animals, they lack any means of self-defense. In essence, they are defenseless against attack. And they are easily led astray. When feeding, sheep can become so consumed with what they are doing, that they can walk right off the edge of a cliff. Sheep can't heal, fend for, or lead themselves.

In Isaiah 53:6 we are given a perfect picture of how God views us. "All of us, like sheep, have strayed away. We have left God's paths to follow our own." At one time we were like wandering, ignorant, stubborn sheep. We had lost our way. We had wandered off the path and gotten lost. We were defenseless, helpless and hopeless. The prophet Isaiah went on to prophesy that God had a solution for those lost sheep: "Yet the LORD laid on him the sins of us all. He was oppressed and treated harshly, yet he never said a word. He was led like a lamb to the slaughter. And as a sheep is silent before the shearers, he did not open his mouth. Unjustly condemned, he was led away" (Isaiah 53:6a-8b NLT). God's solution for lost, wandering sheep was the Good Shepherd. Peter reminds us, "Once you were like sheep who wandered away. But now you have turned to your Shepherd, the Guardian of your souls" (1 Peter 2:25 NLT).

God is our Shepherd. Jesus is our Good Shepherd. We are their sheep. We are needy, prone to wander, inherently restless, lacking in strength, defenseless, directionless, and hopeless if left to our own devices. But God leads us, loves us, guides us, protects us, comforts us, feeds us, and heals us. He sent His Son to die for us because we couldn't save ourselves. His Son became a sheep just like us so that He could be the sacrificial lamb that satisfied the just demands of a holy, righteous God. He died so that we might live. The key to understanding the 23rd Psalm is understanding our role as sheep and our total dependency on God for all that we need and have. It is because of His goodness and unfailing love that we are even alive and that we have a future. Dependency comes hard to most of us. Learning to rely on God is not easy. We have convinced ourselves that self-sufficiency is a virtue. But sheep rely on their shepherd. They trust their shepherd. They listen to their shepherd. They follow their shepherd. They depend on their shepherd for everything. And they are blessed.

Father, give me a sheep-like attitude. Let me continually die to my stubborn need for self-sufficiency and learn to live in total dependence on You. You are my Shepherd. Your Son is my Good Shepherd. All my needs are met in You. Amen

PSALM 23 – DAY 2

Shepherd Wanted.
Based on Psalm 23

I'm just a sheep, but I've got a Great Shepherd.
Thanks to Him, I have everything I need.
He leads me to pastures with abundant grass,
And streams with clean, cold water
Where I find it easy to relax and renew.
He has a reputation for keeping me on the right track.
But even if he has to lead me down a difficult path,
I don't panic or stress, because He's always with me.
He uses the tools of his trade to keep me safe.
It's like God is treating me to a banquet,
Right in front of my enemies.
He honors me, and they can't stand it.
He blesses me, and it drives them crazy.
Throughout my life, God pursues me with His goodness,
He showers me with His unfailing love.
He has made me a permanent guest in His home.

PSALM 23 – DAY 3

Write Psalm 23 in your own words or write a psalm of your own. Be honest and open. Don't be afraid to tell God how you feel, but also include praise for who He is and all that He has done and is going to do in your life.

PSALM 24 – DAY 1

The King of Glory.

Who is the King of glory? The Lord strong and mighty; the Lord, invincible in battle. – Psalm 24:6 NLT

Ultimately, this song is about God. It speaks of His holiness, power, glory, and transcendence. God is not like us. We are not like God. While we have access into His presence because of Christ's death on the cross, we should not waltz in flippantly or arrogantly. We must recognize His holiness and our own sinfulness. God is separate from us. He is the creator and we are His creation. Everything, including us, belongs to Him. We exist by Him and for Him – not the other way around. God is not our personal valet. He is not our life coach or personal trainer. David reminds us that God is not someone who is to be treated lightly or with disdain. Those who seek God and enjoy the benefits of a relationship with Him are those whose deeds are blameless, whose hearts are pure and innocent, and whose lives are not marked by worthless, vain conduct. They recognize that their behavior plays a big part in their ability to enjoy God's blessings.

God is the King of glory. He is deserving of our praise, adoration, worship, wonder, awe, reverence, fear, and respect. He is strong and mighty. He is holy and righteous. He is set apart. He is above all and deserving of all glory and honor. It is God's separateness and our own sinfulness that should make the cross of Jesus Christ special to us. It is Christ's sacrificial death on the cross that allows us – as sinful men and women – to have access to the very throne room of God. It is what He has done that allows us to share in His righteousness and be viewed by God as holy. We can come into His presence, not because WE are blameless and pure in and of ourselves, but because Jesus Christ was blameless and pure on our behalf. Because He took all our sinfulness on Himself at the cross, we inherited His righteousness. As a result, we are seen by God as blameless, innocent, clean, pure, holy and righteous.

And God has given us His Holy Spirit to indwell us and empower us to live holy lives. We have the ability to live righteously and rightly – in spite of the ongoing presence of our sinful natures. We can live by the Spirit or we can live according to the flesh (our sinful nature). We can live in obedience or disobedience. The choice is up to us. Each day we must recognize God's holiness and our own sinfulness. We must remember what Christ has done for us on the cross. We must rest in the fact that we have within us the same power that raised Christ from the dead living in the form of the Holy Spirit. We *can* live holy lives. We *can* say no to sin and yes to God's transformative power in our lives. Our daily desire should be to come into God's presence – recognizing His holiness and our responsibility to treat Him with dignity, honor and respect. Paul put it this way, "And so, dear brothers and sisters, I plead with you to give your bodies to God because of all he has done for you. Let them be a living and holy sacrifice—the kind he will find acceptable. This is truly the way to worship him" (Romans 12:1 NLT). We belong to Him. He paid for us with His own Son's life. We are to give our lives to Him and allow Him to transform us into the likeness of His Son – and in so doing, we honor Him for who He is – the King of glory.

Father, never let me treat You with anything but respect, glory, and honor. Never let me get so casual with You that I lose sight of your holiness. Never let me take for granted that I have access into Your presence because of what Jesus did for me on the cross. You are the King of glory and You deserve my respect, honor, and awe. Amen

PSALM 24 – DAY 2

The King of Glory.
Based on Psalm 24

Not only does the earth belong to the Lord,
So does everything on it, including every single human being.
It is God who separated the land from the sea
When He created the world in the first place.

So who has a right to come into the presence of someone so powerful?
What would allow anyone to be worthy of standing before someone so holy?
Think about it. Only the person who has clean hands and a pure heart!
Someone whose life is not characterized by worthless conduct and lies.
It's that kind of person who will receive God's blessing and justification.
That's the kind of people who seek You, O Lord.

Open up the gates, swing open the doors,
And let the King of Glory in!
How will you know who the King of Glory is?
He is the Lord, powerful and strong,
He is the Lord, who has proven His strength in battle.
So open up the gates, swing open the doors,
And let the King of Glory in!
How will you know who the King of Glory is?
He is the Lord, the leader of the armies of heaven,
He is the King of Glory.

PSALM 24 – DAY 3

Write Psalm 24 in your own words or write a psalm of your own. Be honest and open. Don't be afraid to tell God how you feel, but also include praise for who He is and all that He has done and is going to do in your life.

PSALM 25 – DAY 1

Looking To God.

Lead me by your truth and teach me, for you are the God who saves me. All day long I put my hope in you. – Psalm 25:5 NLT

This is an amazing psalm. Over and over again it reminds us that there is only one place we are to look for help, hope, healing, deliverance, direction, instruction, inspiration, mercy, forgiveness, and love. Whether things are going great or life has taken a turn for the worse, David tells us that, from his experience, God is worth trusting. In fact, all throughout this psalm David uses the Hebrew word *qavah*, which means "to wait, look for, hope, expect."[6] There is a sense of anticipation and expectation built into the word. This is not about some hopeless resignation because there's nothing else we can do. It is an eager expectation based on God's reputation for righteousness, mercy, love, power, forgiveness, and salvation. David doesn't just pray for God's deliverance, he fully expects it.

David had a long-term perspective. He did not let current circumstances cloud or influence his understanding of God's faithful love and ability to deliver at just the right moment. He knew he could trust God to come through for him. But more than just delivering him from trouble, Paul knew God could direct and guide, providing a clear understanding of what path to take in life. David's God didn't just protect his life, He pointed out the way to live a full and meaningful life. David asks God to "show me the right path" (Psalm 25:4 NLT). He isn't just asking God to point it out, but to clearly make it known so that there is no chance of mistake. David asks God to "lead me by your truth and teach me" (Psalm 25:5 NLT). The word translated "lead" carries the idea of God showing David where to place each footstep along the way. And David knows that God's direction comes from God's Word. The amazing thing is that David asks God to teach him. The word David uses for "teach" is the Hebrew word *lamad*, which means

---

[6] Goodrick, Edward W., and John R. Kohlberger III. *The Strongest NIV Exhaustive Concordance.* Grand Rapids: Zondervan, 2004.

to strike with a rod or to chastise. It was a word used in reference to the training or discipline of cattle.[7] David is inviting God to train him, even if God has to use a little physical discipline. When was the last time you asked God to teach you and not spare the pain?

How could David ask such a thing? He knew that his God was holy, just, righteous and good. "The Lord is good and does what is right" (Psalm 25:8 NLT). He "leads with unfailing love and faithfulness" (Psalm 25:10 NLT). David knew that God had his best interest in mind – all the time. Even in his worst moments, David knew that he could turn to God and God would understand, empathize, rescue, restore, teach, guide, discipline, and love him through it all. This psalm reminds us that God is all-powerful, all-knowing, faithful, righteous, merciful, personal, forgiving, and completely worthy of our trust. David looked to God. He kept his eyes focused on God. But we live in a world where it is easy to focus our attention elsewhere. We can easily look to someone or something else to bring us peace, escape from pain, hope, happiness, wisdom, and protection. But nothing we look to other than God can deliver. None of them can give us what we're looking for. They offer empty promises and always leave us with unfulfilled desires. But God delivers. God comes through. God always shows up, so David kept looking up. "My eyes are always on the Lord, for he rescues me from the traps of my enemies" (Psalm 25:15 NLT). Where are you looking today? Why not look up and eagerly wait for God to show up?

Father, this psalm is so rich and jam-packed with insights into Your character. Help them to come alive in my life and experience. I want to look to You, rely on You, rest in You, wait on You, and eagerly hope in You. Because You are my God. Amen

---

[7] Goodrick, Edward W., and John R. Kohlberger III. *The Strongest NIV Exhaustive Concordance.* Grand Rapids: Zondervan, 2004.

PSALM 25 – DAY 2

I Look To the Lord.
Based on Psalm 25

I open up my life to you, O Lord,
Because I trust in you as my God.
Don't let me be disappointed,
So that my enemies might have reason to celebrate.
But then I remember that no one who looks eagerly to you is ever disappointed,
Because disappointment and shame are for those live without faith.

Lord, help me discern the right direction for my life;
Show me the road you want me to follow.
Point me in the right direction using Your Word,
And if necessary, discipline me so that I learn well,
For You are the sole source of my salvation.
That's why I eagerly look to You each and every day!
I ask you to remember Your tender mercy and faithful love,
Which have been around as long as You have.
But I ask You to forget all the sins I have ever committed,
Including the sins of my youth and all my blatant acts of rebellion.
Let Your memory of me be based on Your faithful love,
And for the sake of Your own goodness, not mine.

My God is good and always does the right thing.
He lovingly points out the right path to those who've lost their way through sin.
He's the one who helps people do what's right,
Like bear injuries rather than return them.
He trains them to live according to His way, not the world's.
To those who defend His covenant and His Word,
The ways of the Lord reflect His unfailing love and faithfulness.

I ask you, O Lord, to forgive my extreme depravity,
Not because I deserve it, but for the sake of Your own reputation.

Who is the man that truly fears God?
It is the man for whom God has pointed out the right path to take.
This is the man who will experience a pleasant life,
Impacting the generations to come after them.
This man receives counsel directly from God,
He lets them experience His covenant first-hand.
That's why I keep my eyes focused on the Lord,
Because He delivers me out of the traps of life.

Turn to me and show me Your grace and favor, Lord,
For I am the only one and am in great need.
The stress I feel in my heart is great,
So I ask You to rescue me from them all!
I ask You to see all my troubles and trials,
And to take away all my sins.
Look and see all my enemies,
And how they hate me with violently.
Guard me, O Lord, snatch me away from them!
Don't let me be put to shame, because I run to You for protection.
May the integrity and uprightness of who You are watch over me,
For I look to You with eager hope and expectation.

O God, pay the price to set Your people free from all their troubles.

PSALM 25 – DAY 3

Write Psalm 25 in your own words or write a psalm of your own. Be honest and open. Don't be afraid to tell God how you feel, but also include praise for who He is and all that He has done and is going to do in your life.

PSALM 26 – DAY 1

A Life of Integrity.

Declare me innocent, O Lord, for I have acted with integrity; I have trusted in the Lord without wavering. – Psalm 26:1 NLT

The life of integrity. What exactly is it? David was able to say, "I live with integrity" (Psalm 26:11 NLT). He said that he had acted or walked (lived his life) with integrity. In the Hebrew language the word for integrity is *tom* and it refers to completeness or wholeness. To live with integrity is to live a life that is non-compartmentalized. In other words, there is no such thing as the secular-sacred split. A person who lives in integrity allows the things of God to impact and influence every area of their life, including their home, work, leisure time, recreation, relationships, finances, etc. There is no area in his life for which someone might be able to point their finger and level an accusation of impropriety or un-Christ-like behavior. It is the same idea found in the qualifications for an elder or deacon in 1 Timothy:

> *If someone aspires to be an elder, he desires an honorable position. So an elder must be a man whose life is above reproach. He must be faithful to his wife. He must exercise self-control, live wisely, and have a good reputation. He must enjoy having guests in his home, and he must be able to teach. He must not be a heavy drinker or be violent. He must be gentle, not quarrelsome, and not love money. He must manage his own family well, having children who respect and obey him. For if a man cannot manage his own household, how can he take care of God's church? An elder must not be a new believer, because he might become proud, and the devil would cause him to fall. Also, people outside the church must speak well of him so that he will not be disgraced and fall into the devil's trap. In the same way, deacons must be well respected and have integrity. They must not be heavy drinkers or dishonest with money. They must be committed to the mystery of the faith now revealed and must live with a clear conscience. Before they are appointed as deacons, let them be closely examined. If they pass the test, then let them serve as deacons.* – 1 Timothy 3:1-10 NLT

A life of integrity is not a life of perfection, but simply a life where our motives and attitudes are marked by a desire to do what God would have us do. It carries the evidence of a love for the things of God rather than the things of this world. A person of integrity is willing to trust God with their *whole* life and dedicate every area of their life to His service, not holding back anything for their own selfish pleasures or desires. As David indicates, it is motivated by the unfailing love of God and is a reaction to all that He has done for us. A person of integrity knows their life does not belong to them, but to God. It is not for them to use as they see fit. That is why David said, "I do not spend time with liars or go along with hypocrites. I hate the gatherings of those who do evil, and I refuse to join in with the wicked" (Psalms 26:4-5 NLT). A person of integrity would rather spend time with God and His people than with anyone else. It is a life of separateness and set-apartness, not compromise and convenience. Which is why David could say, "Put me on trial, Lord, and cross-examine me" (Psalm 26:2 NLT). He was willing to allow God to test the purity of his faithfulness and the validity of his integrity.

What about us? Could our integrity stand up to the heat of God's scrutiny? Is our life characterized more by compartmentalization or wholeness? Are there any areas of our life for which we refuse to turn control over to God? Because of the integrity of his life, David found himself standing on firm footing. He was trusting on the integrity of God and placing his hope in Him. He had found God to be faithful and true. God had proven Himself to be anything but compartmentalized in His relationship with and reaction to David. And so David was willing to live all of his life for God's glory. Paul said it this way, "I plead with you to give your bodies to God because of all he has done for you. Let them be a living and holy sacrifice—the kind he will find acceptable. This is truly the way to worship him" (Romans 12:1 NLT). God wants a complete or whole sacrifice – not partial. His Son died to redeem all of us, not part of us. To live a life of integrity is to give God all that I am because His Son gave His life to redeem all of me.

Father, I want my life to be marked by integrity. Not the worldly, human version, but the biblical version. I want every area of my life to be Yours. I know I hold parts back, afraid to let You control them. But continue to lovingly pry my hands off of those areas I hold so dear and let me place them on the altar as a sacrifice to You. Amen

PSALM 26 – DAY 2

A Life of Integrity.
Based on Psalm 26

You be the judge of my life, Lord,
For I have tried to live it right out in front of You — honestly and openly.
I put my confidence in You, so I am not worried.
Take a good, close look at me, Lord,
Test me, prove me, refine me like gold,
To see if there is anything impure in my heart.
I have a constant awareness of Your faithful love,
And I have tried to live my life according to Your Word.
I don't make a habit of hanging out with people of worthless character,
I don't associate with those who attempt to hide their lives from You.
I hate being in the company of those who love evil.
I've got clean hands and a pure heart,
So I can come into Your presence with confidence,
Expressing my thanks to You and telling others of all You've done in my life.
I love being with You, surrounded by Your glory.

Don't include me in the ranks of unrepentant sinners,
Don't punish me like those who live to do evil.
Everything they do, their whole purpose in life is evil,
Even the things that appear good are done for the wrong reasons.
But that's not me. I try to live my life with integrity,
Uncompartmentalized and wholly dedicated to You.
But ultimately, You must ransom and set me free,
You have to be willing to show me mercy,
So that I can find myself standing confidently in Your presence,
Offering praise to You for what You have done.

PSALM 26 – DAY 3

Write Psalm 26 in your own words or write a psalm of your own. Be honest and open. Don't be afraid to tell God how you feel, but also include praise for who He is and all that He has done and is going to do in your life.

PSALMS 27-28 – DAY 1

Waiting On God.

Wait patiently for the LORD. Be brave and courageous. Yes, wait patiently for the LORD. – Psalm 27:14 NLT

Prayer and patience. Two things that don't come easily to most of us. We may pray regularly, but we probably wait for God's answers impatiently. We don't like to wait. We have a hard time understanding God's delays, especially when we've already told Him what we want Him to do. What could He be waiting for? Why doesn't He just go ahead and give us our the answer to our request – just like we shared it? But David had a confidence in God that was based on his understanding of the character of God. In the midst of difficulty, David could experience rest and a lack of fear, because he knew that God would save and protect him. If he found himself surrounded by the enemy and even under attack, he would not fear, but remain confident – because he could trust God. Waiting on God's answer had become second nature to David. The circumstances that surrounded David were only important to David in that they provided him with an opportunity to trust God and spend time in communion with Him. They gave him the chance to talk to God personally and intimately. While he waited for his answer, he just continued to spend time with God. "Hear me as I pray, O Lord. Be merciful and answer me! My heart has heard you say, 'Come and talk with me.' And my heart responds, 'Lord, I am coming.'" (Psalm 27:7-8 NLT).

David wanted more from God than just rescue. He wanted a relationship. He desired to have God teach him, not just bail him out of trouble. He wanted God to lead him, not just provide him with a trouble-free life. David seemed to understand that the trials of life were there to help him turn to and trust in God. They were opportunities for him to watch God work. So he prayed to God. He put his confidence in God. He looked to God as his source of strength and protection. He knew God would provide him with salvation as well as direction. So he was willing to wait patiently on Him. And he could encourage others to do the same. "Wait patiently for the Lord. Be brave and courageous. Yes, wait patiently for the Lord" (Psalm 27:14 NLT). God is faithful. Like a shepherd who lovingly holds his sheep in his protective arms, God carries and cares for us. He is our source of strength, safety, security, and salvation from anything and anyone that comes against us. So why should we be afraid? Why should we become impatient?

Father, what a great reminder of who You are. My fear and impatience are nothing more than a reflection of my own doubt and ignorance of who You really are. I see my troubles as greater than You are. I see my circumstances as too much for You to handle. When I fear and doubt, I am casting dispersions on Your love and faithfulness. I am saying You either won't or can't save me in my time of need. But You are always faithful and loving. Help me to wait patiently and confidently in You. Help me to be brave and courageous because of the reality of who You are. Amen

PSALMS 27-28 – DAY 2

Waiting On God.
Based on Psalm 27

God is the light of my life,
Illuminating my path and making me successful in all I do.
He is my source of salvation, delivering me in times of need.
He is the one I turn to for refuge and protection.
So why in the world would I be afraid of anyone or anything?
Anytime anyone has tried to hurt or harm me, even my enemies,
They have always failed in their mission.
Even if I should ever find myself facing insurmountable odds,
I will have no reason to be fearful.
Even if they decide to attack me, I will keep trusting in God.

I have one simple request from God, one desire:
That He would allow me to enjoy the peace of His presence my whole life.
So that I could be with Him and experience His marvelous grace.
When the bad times come, God will provide me with a place to hide.
I will find refuge and shelter with Him.
As long as I'm with Him, I'm out of reach of my enemies.
I can look down on them with confidence and peace.
So when I am with Him I want to thank Him,
I want to sing His praises and offer my gratitude in appropriate ways.

Please hear me when I call out to You, Lord.
Show me Your mercy by answering my requests.
You've invited me to come into Your presence,
So that's exactly what I am doing.
It would kill me if You ever hid from me,
Or turned away from me in anger.
You've always been there for me.
I am counting on You to never leave me or forsake me,
Because You are my only source of salvation.

Should my own father and mother abandon me,
You would be there to take me in.
Dangers are out there,
So I depend on You to point my life in the right direction, Lord,
To lead me down the right path.
Don't allow those who wish me harm to succeed.
If I didn't believe You would help me,
I would have given up a long time ago.

The best advice I can give anyone is to wait on God.
Eagerly expect Him to act.
It will strengthen your faith and encourage your heart,
As You learn to excitedly anticipate great things from God.

Without God's Help, All Is Hopeless.
Based on Psalm 28

I cry out to You, Lord, because You're my rock,
And I depend on You to answer me.
If you don't, I am no better off than the worst sinner,
I am helpless and doomed to failure.
So I ask You to hear me when I call for help,
Respond when I cry out to You and lift up my hands in need.

I know that without You my fate is the same as everyone else.
I'll be no different than those who are Your enemies,
Or who live to do bad things.
Give them exactly what they deserve, Lord.
They don't honor You or acknowledge Your activity in the world.
But I will kneel before You, Lord,
Because You have heard my prayers.
You are who I turn to for strength and protection.
When I put my confidence in You, I am never disappointed.
That's why I have joy in my heart
And a praise song on my lips.

You alone have the power to save and rescue Your people.
So I ask You to do just that.
Save us, bless us, feed us, and carry us in Your arms forever.

PSALMS 27-28 – DAY 3

Write Psalm 27 in your own words or write a psalm of your own. Be honest and open. Don't be afraid to tell God how you feel, but also include praise for who He is and all that He has done and is going to do in your life.

PSALMS 27-28 – DAY 3

Write Psalm 28 in your own words or write a psalm of your own. Be honest and open. Don't be afraid to tell God how you feel, but also include praise for who He is and all that He has done and is going to do in your life.

PSALM 29 – DAY 1

Give God the Glory.

Acknowledge the Lord, you heavenly beings, acknowledge the Lord's majesty and power!
– Psalm 29:1 NET

How do you honor someone you can't see? How do you recognize and rejoice in the greatness of a God that is invisible? That has always been a problem for the people of God. Abraham had private conversations with God. So did Moses. He even caught glimpses of God's glory in the burning bush and was allowed to see God's back as he passed by him on the mountain. A handful of God's people have had supernatural glimpses of God's glory. For the rest of us, we are left with the task of trying to honor and adequately ascribe to God the glory He so richly deserves. For David, it was quite simple. He saw God all around him. When he looked into the night sky and saw all the stars and planets, he saw the hand of God. They were a reflection of God's glory. After his anointing as God's choice to be the next king of Israel, he spent years running from King Saul and hiding in the wilderness. While sitting in the mouth of a cave in the middle of the rugged mountain landscape, he saw more than his fair share of storms. As he witnessed the lightning flash across the night sky and occasionally strike a tree, shattering it in two; and as he listened to the thunder echo off the canyon walls, shaking the ground beneath his feet, David couldn't help but think of God. To him, the thunder was the very voice of God. It was a reminder of God's incomparable power. That audible "voice" of God was enough to cause David to stand in awe. Seven times in this passage David refers to God's voice. He knew that God had spoken the world into existence. He recognized that God's words carried weight and the sound of His voice was more powerful than the strongest lightning and capable of bringing great destruction or incredible blessing.

David was a king. He understood the concept of power. He knew that the king's word was law. But he also knew that his power was limited and his voice only carried so much weight. But God's voice was limitless in power. God deserved glory and a recognition on the part of both angels and men that He alone is worthy of worship. David begins this psalm by encouraging us to give honor to God for His glory and strength. He reminds us to recognize God for who He is and worship Him accordingly. He alone is King. His voice is powerful and He is worthy of our worship and praise. But then David ends His psalm with a comforting thought. This same great, glorious, powerful, majestic God gives His people strength and blesses them with security. David knew that it wasn't he and his mighty men who protected the people of Israel – it was God. God gave them strength to face their enemies. God gave them strength to withstand adversity. And it was God who blessed them with peace or shalom, not just an absence of conflict, but a sense of completeness, an awareness of well-being and security in the midst of adversity.

The next time a storm rolls into town and you find yourself woken up by the sound of thunder, think about God. When you look out the window and watch the lightning flash across the sky, think about God. You are getting a little glimpse of the incredible power of God. Let it remind you of just how great He is. Let it cause you to give Him the glory He so richly deserves. "Honor the Lord for the glory is his name. Worship the Lord in the splendor of his holiness" (Psalm 29:2 NLT).

Father, Your power is all around us, but we fail to recognize it. We see nature, but we don't see the God behind it. Give me the eyes of David. Help me to see Your presence constantly surrounding me. Let me recognize Your existence in all of life. I want to worship You and honor You for who You are. I want to grow in my awareness of Your power and glory. Open my eyes so that I might see You more clearly each day. Amen

PSALM 29 – DAY 2

Hearing the Voice of God.
Based on Psalm 29

The angels in heaven are to give God what He deserves.
They are to recognize and respond to His glory and power,
Based on His matchless reputation alone.
They are to worship the Lord due to the holiness that cloaks Him like a robe.

God's powerful voice is like the thunder that carries across the ocean in a storm.
His glory and majesty are palpable,
Like thunder over the a huge ocean expanse.
His voice is strong, powerful and unmistakable,
It is majestic and awe-inspiring.
It is more powerful than lightning that splits a tree in two,
Or shatters a full-grown tree into kindling.
His voice can rock the mountains, making them appear to leap about,
Like a calf or a young wild ox.
His voice isn't just heard, it makes an impact,
Like a bolt of lightning striking the earth.
It reaches even into the wilderness,
Leaving an impression wherever it goes.
It is powerful enough to make an impression,
Like lightning that twists trees and wind that leaves the forest leafless.
And the reaction in heaven? They shout, "Glory!"

The Lord is in control of the oceans and the seas,
He is the King who reigns over everything for all time.
And this same King gives His people the strength they need.
He will give them His peace, even in the storm,
Because He is in complete control. He is all-powerful.

PSALM 29 – DAY 3

Write Psalm 29 in your own words or write a psalm of your own. Be honest and open. Don't be afraid to tell God how you feel, but also include praise for who He is and all that He has done and is going to do in your life.

PSALM 30 – DAY 1

Deeply Dependent.

When I was prosperous, I said, "Nothing can stop me now!" Your favor, O Lord, made me as secure as a mountain. Then you turned away from me and I was shattered. – Psalm 30:6-7 NLT

David wrote this psalm as a song to be sung at the dedication of the Temple – an event he would never live long enough to personally witness. But the words of this psalm reflect the heart of David toward his God. He loved God and had a desire to worship Him and honor him with his life. He recognized God's hand in his life over the years and enjoyed a unique vantage point from which to look back and put his life into perspective. He could see the countless times that God had rescued him from his enemies. He could recall the many occasions he had called out to God in sickness or weakness, and God had answered with healing and strength. He remembered the many examples from his life when his actions had angered God, but he also remembered that God had always been quick to extend mercy whenever David returned to Him and repented. David could vividly recall the sleepless nights when he found himself in tears because of hopelessness and helplessness. But morning always seemed to bring with it joy and a sense of peace, because God was there. Then there were those times when all was going well in David's life and his world was rocking along seamlessly and happily. In those times, David tended to get cocky and begin to take himself a little too seriously. He became dangerously independent from God – a threat we all face as believers. Because all was going well in his life, David began to take credit for his life, which led him to take responsibility for his life. He didn't need God, which is what led him to say, "Nothing can stop me now!" He was invincible! Or so he thought. But in looking back, David realizes that it was only the favor of God that allowed him to prosper and thrive. If God removed that favor, David was in trouble and, sadly, he had experienced that reality on more than one occasion in his life. Whenever we get brash and bold enough to believe that we don't need God, He allows us to understand just what that kind of life will look like. Prosperity without God's presence is joyless, meaningless, and in the end, a waste of time. Success without God's favor is like eating cotton candy – lot's of flavor, but of no long-term value for sustaining life.

At those moments in his life when David realized he had begun to take himself too seriously and God too lightly, he repented and cried out for mercy. He begged God to forgive him and restore Him. "Hear me, LORD, and have mercy on me. Help me, O LORD" (Psalm 30:10 NLT). Those are words that our heavenly Father loves to hear from His children. He longs to be there for us, to help us, protect us, give us direction, and love us through providing for us. David knew from experience that God was there to pick us up whenever we're down; to meet needs we have no capacity to meet; to win battles we have no strength to fight, let alone win; and to forgive us when we repent. He replaces our sadness with joy. All He asks is that we replace our independence with dependence and our self-sufficiency with a total reliance upon Him. When we do, we will be able to say along with David, " O LORD my God, I will give you thanks forever!" (Psalm 30:12b NLT).

Father, forgive me for my arrogant independence. Far too often I want to live my life my way and take credit for the successes. But then I want to turn around and blame You for the failures. May I grow increasingly more aware of just how much I need You for everything in my life. And may I never forget that I can take no credit for anything good that happens in my life. It is all a result of Your good favor. Amen

PSALM 30 – DAY 2

I Will Exalt Him.
Based on Psalm 30

I will lift You up, O Lord, because You have always held me up,
And have never given anyone reason to rejoice in my failure.
I cried out to You, and You heard me.
Even in those times when I felt like I was about to die,
You lifted me up and kept me alive, and kept me going.
You gave me hope.
Rejoice in the Lord, all those who follow after Him,
Give Him thanks every time you think about His holiness.
For His anger doesn't last, but His favor does.
You may experience sorrow for a short time,
But with God, it is always followed by joy.
Then there are those times when I got cocky and said,
"Look at all I have done! I am pretty significant!"
But then I always remember that it is You alone who makes me who I am.
I only stand strong because of You.
When I stop relying on You, I stumble and fall.
I find myself in deep trouble without You.
So I cry out to You for help and beg for Your favor.
What would it accomplish if I died?
What good would I be to You dead?
So hear me Lord, and listen to my cry for help.
Do what You have done so many times before.
Turn my sadness into joy, turn my despair into delight.
With that in mind, I will not keep silent, but praise You.
I will spend my whole life giving You thanks for all You have done.

PSALM 30 – DAY 3

Write Psalm 30 in your own words or write a psalm of your own. Be honest and open. Don't be afraid to tell God how you feel, but also include praise for who He is and all that He has done and is going to do in your life.

PSALM 31 – DAY 1

Be Strong!

So be strong and courageous, all you who put your hope in the LORD! – Psalm 31:24 NLT

Why do we fear? Why do we doubt? When we serve a God who is as great as ours is and loves us like He does, what in the world would cause us to ever distrust or doubt Him? Probably our own human weakness and sin. In our limited understanding, we know of no one or nothing that is as strong as God. We have no experience with anyone who is as reliable and trustworthy as God. We tend to judge God based on human standards and our own limitations. If we truly believed God was all-powerful, all-knowing, and all-loving, would we fear as much? Would we doubt as much? Would we worry as much as we do? It seems that a big part of the journey for us as Christ-followers is to learn to trust God more and to fear life less. In this psalm, David seems to ebb back and forth between a strong confidence in God and a wavering doubt. He says, "Save me, for you do what is right" (Psalm 31:1 NLT). He calls God his rock, fortress, and his faithful God. He talks of God's unfailing love and mercy. But then David seems to change tones. He says, "Have mercy on me, LORD, for I am in distress. Tears blur my eyes. My body and soul are withering away. I am dying from grief; my years are shortened by sadness. Sin has drained my strength; I am wasting away from within" (Psalm 31:9-10 NLT). David faces the daily reality of life living in a fallen world. He has to confront wickedness and the influence of sinful people who make it hard to live the life of faith. There is a constant battle between trusting God and living in the midst of difficult circumstances that are constantly attempting to shake our faith in Him. Knowing and serving God do not guarantee us an easy road or a life free from difficulty. But they do promise us a God who loves us enough to care about what is happening to us and is powerful enough to do something about it. David seemed to know that from experience. In spite of his difficulties, he turned to God. He knew where the source of his help and hope was to be found. In God alone. David states confidently, "But I am trusting you, O LORD, saying, 'You are my God!' My future is in your hands" (Psalm 31:14-15a NLT). All David had to do was remember the countless times God had rescued him before, whether it was when the city was under attack and God rescued them from defeat, or God heard David's cry of personal need and answered. God had proven Himself faithful in the past, and David knew God would prove Himself so in the future. He could be trusted. Which is why David could say with confidence, "So be strong and courageous, all you who put your hope in the LORD!"

Father, thank You that You can be trusted. And because You can be trusted, I can be brave and strong. May my courage increase daily as I learn to rely on and trust in You. May I increasingly learn to put my hope in You. Amen

PSALM 31 – DAY 2

I Trust In You.
Based on Psalm 31

I am putting my trust in You, O Lord,
So don't ever let me be disappointed.
Deliver me, because You are righteous.
Please listen to me and rescue me.
Be my rock, my strength, my security. Keep me safe.
You are all those things and more to me,
And because of Your reputation, you will lead and guide me.
You will set me free from the traps that others set for me,
For You are my protector.
I have trusted You with my life,
Because You are my faithful Redeemer.
I can't stand those who buy into worthless lies,
But I trust in You.
I will find joy in your unfailing love and mercy,
Because You saw what I was going through and felt my pain.
You don't give me over to the enemy,
But put me in a place of safety and security.
I am at another one of those times when I need Your mercy,
My eyes are tired and my strength is gone.
It seems like I spend all my time lately in pain and sadness.
Part of it is due to my own sinfulness. It always produces pain.
But then my enemies have played their part as well.
They have just about destroyed my reputation,
Causing even my friends to avoid me like the plague.
I am out of sight and out of mind,
As good as dead, as useless to them as a broken pot.
I hear all the whispers behind my back,
I know what they're plotting against me,
And how they desire to have me out of the way.
But in spite of all this, I trust in You, because You are my God!
You are in complete control of my life,

So rescue me from all those who wish me harm.
Look on me kindly, rescue me because of Your faithfulness.
Don't let me be disappointed, Lord, because I trust in You.
Instead, let those who refuse to trust in You be disappointed.
Silence the liars, the prideful and those who slander with their words.
Your mercy and favor is unlimited, Lord,
And You have plenty to spare for those who love and fear You.
They find safety in Your presence,
Far from those who would attack them physically or verbally.
I offer You praise for all the times You have proven Your faithfulness,
Like that time when the city was under siege from my enemies.
I panicked and concluded that You had left me somehow.
But You heard my cry anyway.
So I want to encourage everyone who loves the Lord to follow Him.
He rewards those who remain loyal to Him,
And He pays back those who arrogantly ignore Him.
So put Your hope in the Lord and stay strong and courageous.

PSALM 31 – DAY 3

Write Psalm 31 in your own words or write a psalm of your own. Be honest and open. Don't be afraid to tell God how you feel, but also include praise for who He is and all that He has done and is going to do in your life.

PSALM 32 – DAY 1

The Joy of Forgiven Sin.

Oh, what joy for those whose disobedience is forgiven, whose sin is put out of sight! –
Psalm 32:1 NLT

One of the inevitabilities of life as a follower of Christ is our own sinfulness. We have inherited a sin nature and it shows up uninvited and without warning on a regular basis in all of our lives. Sometimes our sins are small and appear relatively harmless. Other times, even we are appalled at the extent of our own capability to commit sins that are offensive to most men, let alone God. Our sin natures are always doing battle within us, fighting with the indwelling influence of the Holy Spirit. Paul put it this way, "The sinful nature wants to do evil, which is just the opposite of what the Spirit wants. And the Spirit gives us desires that are the opposite of what the sinful nature desires. These two forces are constantly fighting each other, so you are not free to carry out your good intentions" (Galatians 5:17 NLT). The battle within us is real and the presence of our sin nature is easy to recognize. We see it in the sins we commit on a daily basis, both sins of commission and omission. We don't do the things we should do and we do those things God has forbidden us to do. But here is the good news: God is fully aware of our sin nature. He knows that we are sinners, which is why He sent us a Savior in the form of His own Son. God has set us free from slavery to sin. We no longer HAVE to sin, because we also have a new nature within us. He has given us His Spirit to indwell us, fill us, and empower us to live a life that is no longer sin-prone, but Christ-centered. We now have the capacity to NOT sin. We can say no to sin. "We know that our old sinful selves were crucified with Christ so that sin might lose its power in our lives. We are no longer slaves to sin. For when we died with Christ we were set free from the power of sin" (Romans 6:6-7 NLT).

But the truth is, we still sin, because we still have three things contending against us: Satan, the world, and our own sinful flesh or sin nature. John reminds us, "If we claim we have no sin, we are only fooling ourselves and not living in the truth" (1 John 1:8 NLT). So sin is still inevitable, but it's also avoidable. When we do sin, there is hope. We have forgiveness available to us. We need only confess or admit our sin to God and He offers complete forgiveness. Confession is not telling God something He doesn't already know about us. He knows everything. He sees all our sins. Confession is agreeing with God on the presence of sin in our lives and acknowledging our need for His forgiveness. David said, "I confessed all my sins to you and stopped trying to hide my guilt" (Psalms 32:5 NLT). That word for confessed is *yada* in the Hebrew and it carries the idea of both knowing something and making it known. As we become aware of sin in our lives, God asks us to acknowledge or make it known to Him. That is confession. Attempting to hide it or deny it is ridiculous because God already knows all about it. When we refuse to confess it, all we miss out on is the forgiveness. As part of His sanctifying process in our lives, God is always revealing our sins to us. It is like He is taking a flash light and shining it into the dark recesses of our lives in order to point out the hidden remains of our sin nature that lurk there. When He reveals our sins to us, all He asks is that we agree that we see them, acknowledge or confess their presence to Him, and ask for His forgiveness. And the good news is, that is exactly what we receive. David says, "what joy for those whose record the LORD has cleared of guilt, whose lives are lived in complete honesty!" (Psalms 32:2 NLT).

David loved the forgiveness of God because he knew how much he needed it. He was a sinner just like you and me. He did not always do what God wanted him to do and he sometimes did those things God did not want him to do. But David knew the reality and blessing of confession and forgiveness. And he implores us to live a life of constant confession as well. In fact, he gives us these words from the Lord Himself as a way of encouragement, "I will guide you along the best pathway for your life. I will advise you and watch over you. Do not be like a senseless horse or mule that needs a bit and bridle to keep it under control" (Psalms 32:8-9 NLT). God is guiding and directing us how to live. Part of that process is exposing the sin in our lives so that we might be made aware of it and then confess it to Him. It is for our own good. To refuse to see it, acknowledge it, and confess it would make us like a senseless horse or mule that needs the pain of a bridle and bit to make it do what it is supposed to do. Confession is meant to be comforting. It leads to forgiveness. It frees us from guilt. It restores our relationship with the Father. And it brings us joy. So why wouldn't we confess our sins readily and regularly?

Father, I confess to You that I do not confess often enough. I sometimes try to ignore my sins as if they are not that great. But I know that I need to see them and confess them to You. They are a constant reminder to me of my need for You. I cannot cleanse myself. I cannot sanctify myself. I cannot get rid of my sin by myself. Only You can remove the sin that remains within me. Only You can conquer the sin nature that still does battle with me daily. So I want to learn to confess more regularly and readily, so that I might enjoy the blessing of Your forgiveness.. Amen

PSALM 32 – DAY 2

Forgiven!
Based on Psalm 32

What an amazing fact to know that every sin I commit is forgiven by God!
That every sin I commit against Him is put out of sight and out of mind.
I can rejoice because God has removed all need for guilt and shame,
When I simply choose to live my life in openness and honesty before Him!
But on those occasions when I refuse to admit my own sin,
I am the one who ends up suffering.
Because I belong to Him, I feel Him convicting me throughout the day,
And I get no peace until I acknowledge what He already knows – I have sinned.

But then I come to my senses and choose to confess the truth,
And stop acting as my sin is too insignificant or non-existent.
I finally reach the point where I decide, "It's time to come clean with God!"
And then, amazingly, my sin is forgiven, just like that!

So why wouldn't those who claim to serve God, cry out to God?
Why would they choose to suffer judgment when forgiveness is offered?
God wants to be our protector and provider.
He wants to bless us, not curse us.
He desires to bring us joy, not sorrow.

He says, "I can open your eyes and show you the right way to live,
I'll provide you with all the advice you need.
But you can't be head strong and hold on to your sins,
requiring that I have to do things the hard way, like a stubborn horse needs a bridle."

Those who choose not to follow me can expect trouble in life,
But for those who choose to trust me, they can expect mercy from me.
So do what God say, and rejoice.
Be happy because God forgives sin and gives us pure hearts.

PSALM 32 – DAY 3

Write Psalm 32 in your own words or write a psalm of your own. Be honest and open. Don't be afraid to tell God how you feel, but also include praise for who He is and all that He has done and is going to do in your life.

PSALM 33 – DAY 1

Praise Him Because You Can Trust Him.

For the word of the Lord holds true, and we can trust everything he does. – Psalm 33:4
NLT

Do you trust God? I mean *really* trust Him? If we're honest, we have to
admit that there are a lot of things in our lives that we either refuse to trust
God with or we fear trusting to His care. But David reminds us that we can
trust God with anything and everything. After all, He made everything that
exists in the universe, from the farthest reaches of the solar system to the
tiniest microbe that exists. He created the land and the oceans, and
everything that lives, including you and me. He is greater than the most
powerful nation on the planet. He can easily frustrate their best-laid plans
and bring to nothing all their schemes for glory and power.

And this great, all-powerful God has created a universe in which He loves
righteousness and justice, He loves seeing that it happen, and He is
powerful enough to bring it about. But the key to comprehending and
appreciating the power and justice of God is to have a right relationship
with Him. David knew that the Hebrew people had been chosen by God.
Not because of anything they had done or because they somehow deserved
His selection of them. No, God had chosen them and made them His own.
He had blessed them with His presence and prospered them with His
power, often in spite of their own stubbornness and stupidity. So when
David considers the greatness and the graciousness of God, he can't help
but say "sing for joy to the Lord!" He tells us to praise Him and rejoice in
the fact that we have been chosen by Him. We are to fear Him, honor Him,
respect Him, and rely on His unfailing love. We are to put our hope in Him,
understanding that He alone is who we can trust. Only God can save. Only
God can rescue. Only God can deliver. So we put our trust in Him. Hope is
anticipatory. Hope is expectant. Because hope is based on truth – the reality
that God is faithful, powerful, merciful, and fully capable to accomplish His
will on our behalf. It flows from His unfailing, unceasing, unquenchable
love for us. He loves us. We belong to Him. He will not abandon us or

forget about us. We can trust Him to do what is just and right on our behalf, even when we might not understand or like what is going on at the moment. We can praise Him **preemptively** because we KNOW He is going to come through for us eventually.

*Father, I praise You now for what You are **going** to do, not just for what You've already done. Your grace and mercy to me is guaranteed by Your own character. Your love for me never fails. Your power on my behalf is never limited. So I can praise You now for what You have yet to do. Because You will always do what is right and just. Amen*

PSALM 33 – DAY 2

Worthy of My Praise.
Based on Psalm 33

Everyone who claims to be a follower of God should sing His praises,
Because that's the natural response of those who have been made righteous by Him.
It makes all the sense in the world to praise Him for what He has done.
We should praise Him with all kinds of music,
Making up new songs to celebrate His name and express our joy.
Why? Because every word that comes out of His mouth can be trusted,
And you can count on every single thing He does.
He not only loves justice, He loves making sure justice is done,
And it is always an expression of His unfailing, all-encompassing love.

This is the same God who spoke the universe into existence.
He breathed out and the stars suddenly appeared.
He created the land and the oceans.
So even the whole physical world should stand in awe of God,
And every single person who lives on this planet should fear Him.
For no other reason than that He is the creator-God,
Who formed all that exists with the mere power of His voice.

This same God is greater than any nation.
It is completely up to Him whether their petty plans ever come about.
But His plans are eternal and unstoppable.
His intentions are inevitable and irreversible.
So any nation that worships God has reason to be happy.
Any people who have been chosen by God are truly blessed.

God has a prime vantage point from which to watch all men.
He carefully observes them, considering their actions,
And because He knows their hearts, He knows and understands what they do.
It all boils down to trust.
But even a king can't put all his trust in his army.
A great soldier can't always trust in his own strength.

Even a battle-proven weapon might not come through every time.
But those of us who love and fear God can trust Him.
He watches over every one of us who rely on His unfailing love.
He keeps us from dying prematurely,
Sustaining our lives even in the worst of times.

So we trust our lives to God, waiting for Him.
Because He is the one who helps and protects us.
In the end we will experience true happiness,
Because we have decided to trust in His reputation.
So God, show us Your unfailing love and mercy,
Because we expectantly wait for You to come through.

PSALM 33 – DAY 3

Write Psalm 33 in your own words or write a psalm of your own. Be honest and open. Don't be afraid to tell God how you feel, but also include praise for who He is and all that He has done and is going to do in your life.

PSALM 34 – DAY 1

Discovering God's Goodness – The Hard Way.

By experience you will see that the Lord is good; happy is the man who has faith in him.
– Psalm 34:8 BBE

The goodness of God. We read about it, hear sermons about it, and are encouraged to believe in it. But the truth is, sometimes we doubt it. We may find it easy to sing, "God is so good," but when we find ourselves in times of trouble, we begin to question the validity of that statement. We wonder whether God will come through for us. We waffle and waver in our belief that God has our best interest at heart, and then we begin trying to decide how to deal with our problems on our own. David had moments like this, and Psalm 34 was written after just such an experience. He found himself at odds with King Saul. Things were so bad that the king had tried to kill David with his own hands. Then when the king's own son, Jonathan, questioned his actions, Saul tried to kill him as well. David was forced to run from Saul and go into hiding. This was a difficult time for him, because he had to leave everything he knew and loved behind. It must have been a confusing time for him as well. He had been anointed to be the next king by Samuel, the prophet. God had given him a great victory over Goliath, the Philistine warrior. David had served King Saul in his court and gained a reputation as a mighty warrior. He had married the king's daughter and become best friends with the king's son. Now he was running for his life. None of this made sense to David. He must have questioned the goodness of God. He was so confused that he ran away to the city of Gath, the hometown of Goliath, the Philistine he had killed with nothing but a sling and a stone. I don't know what David was thinking when he attempted to seek refuge in the city of his enemies, but he found himself in a real predicament. Even they knew of David's reputation and saw him as the next king of Israel. They said, "Isn't this David, the king of the land?" David knew he was in trouble, so to save himself, he came up with a brilliant strategy. He decided to feign insanity. He began scratching at the doors like a madman complete with drool dripping out of his mouth. Convinced of David's insanity, the king of Gath allowed David to leave unharmed. David ends up hiding in a cave in the wilderness where he was joined by his family and other disenchanted individuals who were chaffing under the reign of King Saul. It was sometime during this period of David's life that he penned Psalm 34.

David had doubted the goodness of God. He had allowed his circumstances to influence his belief in God's inherent goodness and unfailing love. Even though he had been chosen by God and anointed as Saul's successor, David had a hard time comprehending any good coming out of all that was happening to him. He could not see the hand of God behind the difficulties he was experiencing. So he panicked and came up with his own plan. But David was going to learn from experience that God is good – all the time. Because it is only through our experiences that we truly discover the goodness of God. David wase able to say, "The righteous person faces many troubles, but the Lord comes to the rescue each time" (Psalm 34:19 NLT), because he had experienced the truth of this statement in his own life. David was going to have plenty of times in his life where things would not make sense. There would be more than a few occasions when he would find himself under attack, overwhelmed, out of his league, and down on his luck. But he would learn to trust God. He would learn to rely on the goodness of God. God would hear him when he called. God would rescue him out of trouble. God would meet all his needs. God would be close to him regardless of what was happening to him. Through the experiences of life, David would learn the reality and reliability of God's goodness.

Father, You are good. You have never shown Yourself to be otherwise in my life. There have been plenty of times when I have doubted it and, like David, I have come up with my own solution to my problems. But my plans always prove to be a bad substitute for Your goodness. Continue to teach me to trust You regardless of what I see happening around me or to me. Troubles are going to come, but so is help, because You are good. Amen

PSALM 34 – DAY 2

Experience the Goodness of God.
Based on Psalm 34

I am going to praise God constantly,
Because I have plenty of reasons to do so.
My entire life will be a display of God's glory.
Everyone who finds themselves in trouble will be encouraged.

Let's tell of God's greatness together;
And brag about His reputation, fame and renown.
I looked to God for help and He heard me.
He released me from all the fears that controlled and captivated me.
The faces of those who turn to God will be filled with joy, not shame.
I was in a sorry state when I called to God,
And He heard me and rescued me.
God sends His angels to guard those who fear Him,
Surrounding and protecting them.

The goodness of God is something you have to experience.
When you take refuge in God, you discover true joy.
Those who have been chosen by God should fear Him,
Recognizing that He provides all that they need.
Even a ferocious lion gets hungry at times and in need of food.
But everyone who puts their trust in God never does without.

So listen to what I have to say children.
I will teach you what it really means to fear God.
If you want to live a long and successful life,
Learn to control your tongue and watch what you say.
Resist doing what is wrong and instead do what is right.
Do everything to live a life of peace.

God has his eyes on those who love this way.
He listens to their cries for help.
But as for those who live in opposition to God,
He turns away from them,
And everyone forgets they ever existed.
But His people have His full and undivided attention.
He delivers them from every predicament and problem.
When you find yourself heartsick and hopeless, God will be there.
He encourages the discouraged.

The reality is that even the godly will face tough times.
But God will be there to rescue them each and every time.
Because He protects the righteous,
Even keeping their bones from breaking if necessary.

But as for the wicked, they can expect everything to go wrong.
Those who are God-haters will be punished.
But those who love and serve God will be set free.
Instead of condemnation, they will find refuge.

PSALM 34 – DAY 3

Write Psalm 34 in your own words or write a psalm of your own. Be honest and open. Don't be afraid to tell God how you feel, but also include praise for who He is and all that He has done and is going to do in your life.

PSALM 35 – DAY 1

Turning To God.

O LORD, you know all about this. Do not stay silent. Do not abandon me now, O Lord. Wake up! Rise to my defense! Take up my case, my God and my Lord. – Psalm 35:22-23 NLT

This is a difficult psalm. It is one of four imprecatory psalms in which the writer asks God to pour out judgment on his enemies. The words are harsh and come across as vindictive. They don't seem to fit in with the New Testament concepts of loving our enemies and turning the other cheek. David is calling down curses from God on those who oppose him. He asks God to destroy them. So what are we supposed to do with this information? Are we to use this psalm as a pattern for our own prayer lives? Does the content of this psalm provide us with a model for how to respond to those who oppose us or try to do us harm? I think the answer is no.

The real lesson of this psalm is that life is difficult. Even David, the king of Israel and the man who was known as a man after God's own heart, found himself facing difficult situations. He was falsely accused, unjustly attacked, and under constant threat of betrayal from both within and without. We must always remember that David was writing as the king of Israel. He was the anointed, God-appointed leader of the nation and was responsible for opposing all those who stood against God and His people. David's job as king was to defeat the enemies of Israel and defend the people of God. As the king, he represented God and was the target for attack by all those who refused to acknowledge Yahweh as the one true God. David is obviously frustrated and fearful. He is tired of the constant attacks on his leadership and his person. He is weary of all the false accusations and clandestine attempts to dethrone and defeat him. He is frustrated by the ill treatment he receives from those to whom he has shown mercy and grace. In his frustration, David calls out to God to turn the tables and give these individuals a taste of their own medicine.

The real key to understanding this psalm is not based on *what* David asks to be done, but on *who* he asks to do it. David is the king. He could have taken matters into his own hands and given these people just what he prescribes in this psalm. He was a warrior and had a strong army at his disposal. He was the ultimate judge in the land and could have enacted judgment and meted out justice as he saw fit. David could have taken matters into his own hands and solved all these problems in his own way. But instead he called out to God. He appealed to the ultimate judge of all men and asked Him to act as his advocate and protector. This psalm is brutally honest and paints a very clear picture of the pain and frustration that David felt. It provides an accurate glimpse into the life of this man who tried to love and serve God all his life. He shares his heart with God, honestly opening up about his feelings. He holds nothing back. But in the end, David places all of this in the hands of God. He knows the solution to his problems is going to come from one source only: God. He knows victory comes from God. He knows rescue comes from God. He knows justice comes from God. And he knows that God knows everything that is going on in his life. So he asks God to come to his defense, to take up his case and declare him innocent. David is willing to wait on God. Yes, he struggles with what appears to be God's apparent delay in answering, but he waits nonetheless. He gives God his cares and concerns and trusts Him to do what is right. Why? Because he knew that "Great is the Lord, who delights in blessing his servant with peace? (Psalm 35:27 NLT).

Father, life can be hard. People can be difficult. Sometimes I am tempted to take matters into my own hands in an attempt to solve my problems. But help me to turn to You instead. You are my advocate, protector, and rescuer. You know what is best and You always do what is right. Amen

PSALM 35 – DAY 2

In This Together.
Based on Psalm 35

Lord, I have a lot of enemies,
But only because I serve You.
So I ask You to stand against them,
And fight those who oppose me because they oppose You, too.
I need You to stand beside me in battle,
And use every weapon at Your disposal.
I long to hear you say, "I will save you!"
Disappoint and humiliate those who are trying to do me in,
May the plans of those who want to harm me fail.
Scatter them to the four winds,
Blow them away through Your power.
Send one of Your angels to pursue them,
And may the path they take be dark and slippery.
I don't deserve what they are doing to me.
I did them no wrong, but they are trying to trap me.
So give them a taste of their own medicine!
Let what they desire for me happen to them.
Let them experience exactly what they have planned for me.

I know that I am going to be able to rejoice in spite of all this,
Because I am sure of Your salvation. You will rescue me.
And when You do, I will praise You, saying,
"Who is like You, O Lord,?
Is there anybody else who can deliver the weak from the strong?
Does anybody else have the ability to protect the helpless and poor?"

So here I am, surrounded by those who testify falsely against me.
I am being accused of things I have not done.
I have done good and am being repaid with evil.
All of it leaves me literally sick.
The irony is, when my enemies were sick, I showed compassion.

I grieved for them, fasted for them, and prayed for them.
I treated them like family, even feeling sadness over their condition.
But now that I am the one in trouble, they are happy!
They even join in against me.
In fact, I have enemies whose names I don't even know!
They attack me relentlessly.
They're out to destroy my reputation.
Lord, to be honest, sometimes it feels like you see all this,
But You do nothing about it.
I really need you to rescue me and protect me.
When You do, I will tell everyone of my gratefulness,
I will sing Your praises to everyone I meet.
All I ask is that You keep my enemies from having a party at my expense.
Don't give those who have no reason to hate me, a chance to smile at my misfortune.
These people are not godly.
Instead of peace, they pursue deception and discord,
They long to destroy me, saying, "We've got you this time!"

Lord, I am not telling You anything you don't already know.
I am just asking You to act,
To do something about my situation.
I am asking You to stand up and defend me,
To act as my defender, because You are my God.
I am looking to You for justice,
So that You might declare me innocent.
When my enemies laugh at my failure, they are laughing at You,
Because I belong to You and You are my God.
So don't allow our enemies to say, "We've succeeded, we've brought him down!"

I look forward to the day when You act,
When those who find pleasure in my sorrow are disappointed.
They stand over me in victory now,
But one day the roles will be reversed.
Those who love You and serve You like I do
Will all be able to say, "God is great!
He finds great pleasure in protecting and providing for His children."
I know that one day I am going to be able to rejoice in Your justice,
And praise You constantly for what You have done.

PSALM 35 – DAY 3

Write Psalm 35 in your own words or write a psalm of your own. Be honest and open. Don't be afraid to tell God how you feel, but also include praise for who He is and all that He has done and is going to do in your life.

PSALM 36 – DAY 1

A Stark Contrast.

For you are the fountain of life, the light by which we see. – Psalm 36:9 NLT

In this psalm, David compares the wicked with God. Both are realities in his life. As the king of the nation of Israel he is surrounded by enemies – both within and without. He gets to see and experience firsthand the attitudes and actions of the wicked as they interact with him on a daily basis. Of course, David is using the literary device of hyperbole to make his point about the wicked – but only slightly. He speaks of their hearts being filled with wickedness. In fact, they're so blinded by pride, they can't even see how wicked they really are. They have no fear of God and everything they say and do is perverted by their own sin, so that they are incapable of doing anything good or wise. In fact, not a single one of their actions is good at any time. They can't even sleep at night because they're so busy dreaming up more evil things to do the next day. From David's perspective it is as if they couldn't stop doing evil even if they wanted to. And while much of this is exaggerated, there is a certain degree to which it is true. Those who do not know Christ or enjoy a relationship with God through Him are controlled by sin. They are slaves to sin (Romans 6:19). They are incapable of doing what is right or righteous in God's eyes. This does not mean that they can't do any good, but that the good they do will not earn them favor or merit in God's eyes. Isaiah put it this way, "We are all infected and impure with sin. When we display our righteous deeds, they are nothing but filthy rags. Like autumn leaves, we wither and fall, and our sins sweep us away like the wind" (Isaiah 64:6 NLT). So in a way, David was right. The wicked – those who do not believe in God – are incapable of doing anything good. They are controlled by and enslaved to sin.

But then David addresses the other reality in his life: God. While the wicked seemed to surround David and impact his life on a daily basis – so did God. David describes God's unfailing love or mercy, His unbelievable steadfastness or faithfulness, His justice and righteous judgments, and His ever-present salvation, care, provision and protection. David says that God is THE "fountain of life, the light by which we see" (Psalm36:9 NLT). God is not only the source of initial life, but makes possible every breath we take, every second we live on this earth. And that is true not only of us as His children, but of every single person who lives, including the wicked. God provides us with light so that we can see. In the Hebrew verse nine literally says, "In thy light we see light." It is as if David is saying that it is only in the illuminating presence of God's glory that we gain the capacity to see things as they really are. The wicked can't see their own wickedness. But when we stand in the light of God's glory, we see just how sinful we really are.

All this reminds me of the opening verses of John 1. "In the beginning the Word already existed. The Word was with God, and the Word was God. He existed in the beginning with God. God created everything through him, and nothing was created except through him. The Word gave life to everything that was created, and his life brought light to everyone. The light shines in the darkness, and the darkness can never extinguish it" (John 1:1-5 NLT). But John goes on to say, "He came into the very world he created, but the world didn't recognize him. He came to his own people, and even they rejected him" (John 1:10 NLT). The Light of the world came into the world to dispel the darkness, but those who lived in the world rejected Him. They didn't want their darkness exposed. They didn't want the Light to illuminate and eliminate their darkness. "But to all who believed him and accepted him, he gave the right to become children of God. They are reborn – not with a physical birth resulting from human passion or plan, but a birth that comes from God" (John 1:12-13 NLT).

With David we can say, "Pour out your unfailing love on those who love (know) you; give justice those with honest (righteous) hearts" (Psalm 36:10 NLT). We have had our darkness exposed, our sins forgiven and our hearts transformed by the Light of the world. We were once just like those David describes in the opening verses of this psalm. But because of the grace, mercy and goodness of God, we have been given a second chance. We have drunk from the river of delights, enjoy shelter in the shadow of His wings, and are red from the abundance of His house.

Father, we are surrounded by those who love darkness more than light and wickedness more than righteousness. But we used to be the same way. And we would still be that way if it were not for the gracious gift of Your Son. May we learn to love the Light and increasingly appreciate how it exposes our own sin. You are always transforming us into the likeness of Christ and that takes the exposure of our sin nature. It isn't always fun to see, but it's a necessary part of the transformative process. Thank You for Your patient, loving care for us. Amen

PSALM 36 – DAY 2

No Comparison.
Based on Psalm 36

The wicked are rotten to the core,
Even their hearts give them evil advice.
There is not an ounce of the fear of God in them.
They are so puffed up by arrogant pride
That they can't even see the extent of their wickedness.
Even what comes out their mouths is worthless and untrustworthy.
They are too lazy to do what is wise and good.
Even at night they lie awake dreaming up more wickedness.
His whole life stands for the wrong things, refusing to turn from evil.

But God, You are nothing like that.
Your mercy and faithfulness are as limitless as the heavens.
Your righteousness is as immovable as a mountain.
Your judgments are as deep as the oceans.
Your mercy is of great value,
Every person who has ever been born can find refuge under your wings.
They will find themselves completely satisfied,
Because Your house is well-stocked.
You will satisfy their thirst with water from the Your river of luxury,
For the very spring of life begins with You.
You are the Light that makes it possible for men to see.

Draw out Your mercy like water from a river
And share it with those who know You.
Share your righteousness with those whose hearts are right with You.
Don't let the prideful get to me or the wicked shake my confidence,
Because the day is coming when the wicked will fall, never to rise again.

PSALM 36 – DAY 3

Write Psalm 36 in your own words or write a psalm of your own. Be honest and open. Don't be afraid to tell God how you feel, but also include praise for who He is and all that He has done and is going to do in your life.

PSALM 37 – DAY 1

Don't Worry About The Wicked.

Put your hope in the Lord. Travel steadily along his path. He will honor you by giving you the land. You will see the wicked destroyed. – Psalm 37:34 NLT

It's hard not to worry about the wicked. They're all around us. Many of them are in positions of power and influence in our country. Others are considered celebrities and stars. They write books, have their own TV shows, create music and art, and define what is "in" when it comes to everything from clothing to hair styles. The wicked come in all shapes and sizes, and their wickedness is not always readily apparent or easily recognized. They seem to be living lives marked by success, happiness, affluence and popularity. So it's sometimes easy to envy them or to desire to be like them. But David tells us not to worry about the wicked or envy them, because their days are numbered. Yet we often find ourselves getting angry over the apparent lack of justice when it comes to some of these people. They prosper in spite of lifestyles that are marked more by sin than anything else. David reminds us that "it is better to be godly and have little than to be evil and rich" (Psalm 37:16 NLT). To drive the point home, David provides us with a running contrast between the wicked and the godly. He paints a clear and powerful picture of the stark difference between these two lifestyles.

The wicked will soon fade.
But the godly will find shelter in Him.
The wicked will soon wither.
But the godly will never slip from His path.
The wicked will be destroyed.
But the godly will be rescued by God.
The wicked will disappear.
But the godly will trust in the Lord and do good.
The wicked will be gone.
But the godly will never fall.
The wicked plot against the godly.

But God will take care of the godly because they are innocent.
The wicked snarl at them in defiance.
But God will expose the justice of the cause of the godly.
The wicked draw their swords and string their bows.
But God is the fortress of the godly.
The wicked kill the poor and oppressed.
But the godly live in peace and prosperity.
The wicked slaughter those who do right.
But the Lord directs the steps of the godly.
The strength of the wicked will be shattered.
But the godly will be taken care of by God.
The wicked will die.
But the godly will possess the land.
The wicked will disappear like smoke.
But the godly will never be abandoned.
The wicked borrow and never repay.
But the godly give generous loans to others.
The children of the wicked will die.
But the children of the godly are a blessing.
The wicked wait in ambush for the godly.
But God will honor the godly by giving them the land.
The wicked look for an excuse to kill the godly.
But God teaches the godly right from wrong.
The wicked will not succeed.
But the godly will live safely in the land and prosper.
The wicked will be destroyed.
But a wonderful future awaits the godly.
They will appear to flourish, then are gone.
But the godly will not be disgraced in hard times.
The wicked have no future.
But a wonderful future awaits the godly.

As believers we are to put our hope in God. We are to confidently and faithfully trust the path He has chosen for us to follow and not worry about what might appear to be the unfair advantages of the ungodly. God is a just God and He will deal with them in His own way and in His own time. I can leave them in God's hands and concentrate on honoring Him with my life and trusting Him with my future. He will not let the wicked succeed or the godly be condemned. He has it all under control. So don't worry.

Father, thanks for this timely reminder from the pen of David. The wicked have always been around and they have always given Your people cause for consternation and concern. They appear so happy and so together. They seem to be getting away with their lifestyle of open rebellion to You, but You are not done yet. You are a just and righteous God who will make sure that all things are taken care of rightly and justly. They will not escape Your notice or Your judgment. I can leave them in Your hands and rest in the knowledge that You have me securely in Your loving grasp as well. Amen

PSALM 37 – DAY 2

No Comparison.
Based on Psalm 37

Don't waste your energy getting angry about the wicked,
And getting jealous when you see evil people seemingly prosper.
They'll all be gone soon enough.
Their "beauty" is temporary, their day in the sun won't last.

But instead, put your trust in God and concentrate on doing what is right.
That's the key to a good and truly prosperous life.
Keep your eyes focused on God and enjoy His presence,
Make Him your highest priority and He will satisfy you completely.

Give every decision of your life to Him,
Trust it all to Him and He will make things happen.
Your life will reflect His righteous activity,
And His justice will be readily apparent.

Just learn to rest in His presence,
Patiently, expectantly waiting for Him to act.
Quit comparing your life to the godless who seem to be winning.
Stop getting angry because it appears their sin seems to lead to success.

Calm down! Let go of your anger!
Losing your temper never accomplishes anything good.
Those who oppose God get nothing in the end,
But those who trust Him will inherit it all!

Those who oppose God will be gone soon enough.
You'll look around expecting to see them, but they'll be gone.
Instead, you'll find the "losers" of the world enjoying success,
Living peacefully and prosperously.

Right now the godless plot against the godly.
They defiantly oppose everything they stand for,
But none of it concerns God.
He simply laughs, knowing their day of judgment is coming.

The godless attempt to do battle with God.
They attack the poor and needy,
They try to destroy those who live according to God's standards.
But in the end, it's their own destruction they're bringing about.
Their plans will end up backfiring on them.

Here's a peace of advice:
It's better to follow God and live with less,
Than to be wealthy and try to live without God.
The very things the godless put their hope in will fail them,
But God takes care of those who love and trust Him.

There's not a single day of your life God doesn't know about.
He knows your present and your future.
He will not let you down in the hard times,
And nothing is going to happen that He isn't prepared for.

But as for the godless, they will suffer and die.
Their future holds nothing but destruction,
And they are destined to disappear like smoke.

These people are greedy and dishonest.
But the godly are generous to a fault.
God will bless the one and curse the other.

He guides those who follow Him,
Taking joy in directing every detail of their lives.
Yes, they occasionally stumble, but God keeps it from being life-threatening.
Because He holds them in His hands.

I have lived a long time,
But in all those years I have never seen God abandon His own.
I have never seen their children destitute because God failed them.

It's the godly who end up generously sharing what they have with others,
And their children end up following in their footsteps.

So if you want to enjoy the blessings of God,
Turn your back on doing wrong and do good instead.
God loves justice and He will never take His eyes off His own.

He has a secure future in store for the His children,
But the children of the godless have only death to look forward to.
The children of God are here for the long haul.

The godly are able to provide wise counsel,
Teaching the difference between right and wrong.
They base their decisions on the Word of God,
And as a result, their lives have a firm foundation.

The godless spend all their time trying to destroy the godly,
Devising ways to eliminate them from the face of the earth.
But God will never let their plans succeed
Or allow His children to face undeserved condemnation.

Put your hope and trust in God.
Live your life according to His standards,
And you will inherit all He has in store for you.
You will live to see the day when the godless are no more.

In all my years of living, I have seen the wicked flourish like a tree,
But I have also seen them disappear unexpectedly.
I looked around expecting to find them and they were gone!

So instead of worrying about the wicked,
Turn your attention to the godly, to those who do what is right.
Those who love what God loves have a great future ahead of them.
But the godless will end up being destroyed,
Their future is not so pleasant.

God saves the godly,
He provides them with protection in times of trouble.
He comes alongside them, saving them from the godless,
Providing shelter and security from all those who would do them harm.

PSALM 37 – DAY 3

Write Psalm 37 in your own words or write a psalm of your own. Be honest and open. Don't be afraid to tell God how you feel, but also include praise for who He is and all that He has done and is going to do in your life.

PSALM 38 – DAY 1

Sin, Sorrow and Confession.

But I confess my sins; I am deeply sorry for what I have done. – Psalm 38:18 NLT

We are not told what David's sin was, but he clearly articulates what he believes to be the fallout of that sin. David is suffering greatly both physically and emotionally. He sees his circumstances as directly related to his sin and as a rebuke from God. Crying out to God he says, "Because of your anger, my whole body is sick; my health is broken because of my sins. My guilt overwhelms me – it is a burden to heavy to bear" (Psalm 38:3-4 NLT). David clearly understands the concept that God, because He is just, must punish sin and that sin has consequences. There is discipline involved when sins are committed. As children of God we are not allowed to sin freely and without consequence. If we belong to God, our sin produces guilt. His Spirit convicts us of our sin and produces within us those same feelings that David had. He speaks of God's rebuke and discipline. He uses words like crushing, broken, grief, crushed, anguish and pain. And he attributes it all "because of my foolish sins" (Psalms 38:5 NLT).

Speaking of this conviction of sin, C. H. Spurgeon states, "God's law applied by the Spirit to the conviction of the soul of sin, wounds deeply and rankles long; it is an arrow not lightly to be brushed out by careless mirthfulness, or to be extracted by the flattering hand of self righteousness."[8] David was not going to be able to escape the loving discipline of God by simply finding something to distract him. He could avoid it for a time, but his sin, if left unconfessed, would continue to haunt him and leave him longing for relief. Conviction is designed to lead to confession. Conviction ignored will only lead to continued sorrow. It will eat away at you from the inside. That's why confession is so important. It is the anecdote for conviction, guilt and shame. John reminds us, "But if we confess our sins to him, he is faithful and just to forgive us our sins and to cleanse us from all wickedness" (1 John 1:9 NLT). In Psalm 38, the word that David uses that is translated "confess" in the *New Living Translation* is

---

[8] Charles H. Spurgeon, *The Treasury of David*, Volume 1, Psalm 38, The Spurgeon Library, www.spurgeon.org

actually the Hebrew word, נָגַד (*nagad*), which means "to tell or declare." He says that he avows, acknowledges or confesses the sins for which he has been convicted. He gets them out in the open with God. The truth is, God already knows what David has done, and is only waiting for David to acknowledge his guilt before Him. He must agree with God that what he has done is wrong and simply admit it openly. Spurgeon says that this process of confession is therapeutic and healing. "When open confession is good for the soul. When sorrow leads to hearty and penitent acknowledgment of sin it is blessed sorrow, a thing to thank God for most devoutly. *I will be sorry for my sin.* My confession will be salted with briny tears. It is well not so much to bewail our sorrows as to denounce the sins which lie at the root of them. To be sorry for sin is no atonement for it, but it is the right spirit in which to repair to Jesus, who is the reconciliation and the Saviour. A man is near to the end of his trouble when he comes to an end with his sins."[9]

But an important part of confession is sorrow. David says, "I am deeply sorry for what I have done." Confession without sorrow is simply regret or remorse. You may regret your sins because it has produced pain and discipline, but that is not true confession. Confession simply as a means to escape coming punishment is not enough. There must be sorrow for the sin we have committed and not just sorrow for the discipline we are enduring. A child my say he's sorry for something he has done, but it may be motivated by a desire to escape further punishment. It may have nothing to do with a sorrow over having offended his parents. The same can be true with us. In his letter to the Corinthian church, Paul talks about a letter he been moved to send addressing a sin with which they were struggling. He says, "I am not sorry that I sent that severe letter to you, though I was sorry at first, for I know it was painful to you for a little while. Now I am glad I sent it, not because it hurt you, but because the pain caused you to repent and change your ways. It was the kind of sorrow God wants his people to have, so you were not harmed by us in any way. For the kind of sorrow God wants us to experience leads us away from sin and results in salvation. There's no regret for that kind of sorrow. But worldly sorrow, which lacks repentance, results in spiritual death" (2 Corinthians 7:8-10 NLT). The kind of sorrow God wants us to experience leads us away from sin and results in salvation. David was deeply sorry for his sins. He confesses it to God and asks Him to forgive and restore him. He knows that only God can bring the physical, emotional and spiritual healing he needs. He cries out to God,

---

[9] Charles H. Spurgeon, *The Treasury of David*, Volume 1, Psalm 38, Bible Study Tools, www.biblestudytools.com

"Do not abandon me, O Lord. Do not stand at a distance, my God. Come quickly to help me, O Lord may savior" (Psalm 38:21-22 NLT).

Father, they say confession is good for the soul. And nothing could be more true than when it comes to sin in the life of the believer. When we sin, the Spirit convicts our soul and creates in us a holy discontentment and discomfort. Like David, we grow increasingly unhappy with our condition, feeling guilt and shame for what we have done. But You are simply using that conviction to lead us to confession, in order that You might forgive and restore us. Give us an increasing hatred for sin and a willingness to acknowledge its presence in our lives as soon as it shows up. Help us respond quickly to the Spirit's prompting and confess our sin with godly sorrow because we have offended You, our heavenly Father and holy God. Amen

PSALM 38 – DAY 2

Conviction, Confession and Comfort.
Based on Psalm 38

Lord, I beg you not to correct me in anger,
Or discipline me when You're furious with me.
Your arrows of punishment have struck hard and deep,
And I can feel Your hands pressing down on me.
I'm literally sick because of the effects of Your anger on me.
But it all because of the guilt of my own sin.
I'm literally drowning in guilt,
It's all too much for me to handle.
My wounds make me offensive to others,
All because of my own foolishness.
My sin has left me burdened down in brokenness,
I spend my whole day in mourning.
I am humiliated and it is affecting my health.
I am numb and emotionally crushed,
My heart groans in pain and sadness.

But Lord, You know what I long for.
My groans are not hidden from You.
My heart longs, my strength fades,
And any ability to view life with hope diminishes daily.
Everybody avoids me like I had the plague,
Even my own family,
But not my enemies.
They continue to lay traps for me,
Devising ways to do me harm,
Spending their entire days making plans to do me in.

But I might as well be deaf and dumb.
I can't hear what they're saying or speak up in my own defense.
I simply choose to ignore them and say nothing.
Because I am waiting on You God.

I know You are going to answer me.
I have prayed to You for deliverance,
Because otherwise my enemies will win,
And they will gloat over me in victory.

I am ready to give up because my pain is constant.
So I acknowledge my own guilt,
And I am anxious about the effects of my sin.
My enemies are alive and strong,
And their numbers seem to grow daily.
When I do them good, they return the favor with evil,
They can't stand what I stand for.
So I beg You not to forget about me, O Lord!
Hurry up and bring me salvation!

PSALM 38 – DAY 3

Write Psalm 38 in your own words or write a psalm of your own. Be honest and open. Don't be afraid to tell God how you feel, but also include praise for who He is and all that He has done and is going to do in your life.

PSALM 39 – DAY 1

Hope In the Heat.

And so, Lord, where do I put my hope? My only hope is in you. – Psalm 39:7 NLT

David is going through some kind of difficulty. He is under a great deal of pressure and believes that what he is suffering is from the hand of God and due to sin in his life. He is upset and frustrated about it, but has chosen not to complain about his circumstances in the hearing of men – especially the ungodly. He knows that to do so would cast dispersions upon God's grace and goodness. So he just remains silent. But that doesn't stop the emotional turmoil taking place inside his head and heart. He says, "the turmoil within me grew worse. The more I thought about it, the hotter I got, igniting a fire of words" (Psalm 39:2-3 NLT). When David did finally speak up, he chose to take it directly to the Lord. He expressed his thoughts to the one who could do something about it. But instead of complaining, David asked God for perspective. He asks God to "remind me how brief my time on earth will be. Remind me that my days are numbered – how fleeting my life is" (Psalm 39:4 NLT). David was asking God to help him keep his life in the proper perspective, never forgetting that eternity is our future, not this temporary condition we call life. In God's grand scheme, our lives are but a breath, a fleeting moment on the eternal timeline. Yet we put all our emphasis on the here and now and forget about the hereafter. We spend all our time rushing around attempting to accomplish things that only end in insignificance. We work hard to accumulate wealth and then end up having to leave it behind when we go. You can see where David's son, Solomon, got the perspective on life he shared in the book of Ecclesiastes: "I came to hate all my hard work here on earth, for I must leave to others everything I have earned" (Ecclesiastes 2:18 NLT). Solomon also shared David's perspective on wealth. "Then I observed that most people are motivated to success because they envy their neighbors. But this, too, is meaningless – like chasing the wind (Ecclesiastes 4:4 NLT).

But David had decided a long time before he wrote this Psalm to put his hope and trust in God. He had placed his life in God's hands. In fact, he owed his life to God. Without God, David would still be shepherding sheep instead of shepherding the people of Israel. Whatever David was going through, he knew that ultimately it had to pass through the hands of God to get to him. He says, "I am silent before you; I won't say a word, for my punishment is from you" (Psalm 39:9 NLT). David viewed his condition as God-ordained and therefore he took his problem to the source. He believed that his punishment was due to sin in his life and knew that only God could forgive his sin and relieve his suffering. In verse 8 David asks God to "pluck him out of" his sin, to deliver him from his own transgressions. He knows that only God can bring relief from the pain he is suffering. So he asks God to hear his cries, to restore his joy, and to give him relief in order that he might spend whatever days he has on this planet in a right relationship with Him. And isn't that what this is all about? It isn't the accumulation of toys and the gaining of fame. It isn't about comfort and ease, earning and spending, competing and winning. It is about the joy of a right relationship with God. Money can't buy that. When we are not right with God, nothing is right. And nothing can make it right, except getting restored to a right relationship with Him.

Father, what a wonderful reminder that life is all about living for You and with You. The pain and suffering we experience is nothing more than a reminder of our dependence upon and need for You. Keep me focused on You and nothing else. May I desire a right relationship with You more than anything else in the world. Amen

PSALM 39 – DAY 2

Life From An Eternal Perspective.
Based on Psalm 39

I said to myself, "I'm going to be careful about how I live my life.
When I'm around the ungodly, I'm going to watch what I say, so that I don't end up
sinning."
But even when I kept my mouth shut, not even saying anything good,
I found myself getting stirred up inside.
The more I thought about it, the angrier I got,
Until I couldn't take it anymore, and the words spewed out.

Lord, help me comprehend that my life has an end,
That the number of days that I'm going to live are nothing to You.
At best, my life is like a vapor from Your perspective.
The importance we put on our lives is empty and vain.
We waste our time getting upset,
Worrying about all the money we have accumulated
Because we don't even know who will spend it when we're gone.
So where do I put my hope?
I put all my expectations in You.
I ask You to deliver me from living a life of rebellion against You.
Don't let my life be a joke to people who live like fools.
There was a time in my life when I kept my mouth shut
Because You were doing a number on me.
I ask that You remove Your hand of discipline,
Because I am totally spent.
Your punishment disciplines mankind for sin.
You destroy their self-centered self-absorption
Like a moth destroys a beautiful garment.
We're all just a fleeting fog, here one day, gone the next.
So listen to my prayer, Lord!
Hear my cry for help!
Don't be at peace about my tears!

I am a temporary inhabitant here,
A stranger living in a strange land where I don't belong,
Just like my fathers before me.
Take notice of me, smile on me,
Before my life finally comes to an end.

PSALM 39 – DAY 3

Write Psalm 39 in your own words or write a psalm of your own. Be honest and open. Don't be afraid to tell God how you feel, but also include praise for who He is and all that He has done and is going to do in your life.

PSALM 40 – DAY 1

The Best Advertising Is A Satisfied Customer.

I have not kept the good news of your justice hidden in my heart; I have talked about your faithfulness and saving power. I have told everyone in the great assembly of your unfailing love and faithfulness. – Psalm 40:10NLT

When was the last time you told someone else what God has done for you? And I'm not talking about sharing about how you came to faith in Christ. This is about relating to others how God is active in your life accomplishing things that only He could do. David starts out this psalm talking about a time in the not-so-distant past when he found himself patiently waiting on God to help him. And then he says, "he turned to me and heard my cry. He lifted me out of the pit of despair, out of the mud and the mire. He set my feet on solid ground and steadied me as I walked along. He has given me a new song to sing, a hymn of praise to our God" (Psalm 40:1-3 NLT). David was singing God's praises for what He had done in his life. And the result of David's public relations campaign for God? "Many will see what he has done and be amazed. They will put their trust in the Lord" (Psalm 4):3b NLT).

I am convinced that many more people would come to a saving knowledge of Jesus Christ if the followers of Christ had more to say about Him. If we had more to share about what God has done in our lives lately and how Christ is transforming our lives daily, it would give our claims regarding the value of salvation credibility. At this point, so many unbelievers are asking those of us who claim to be followers of Christ and believers in God, "What has He done for you lately?" And if they asked you that question, what would your answer be? What would you tell them? David said, "I have told all your people about your justice. I have not been afraid to speak out, as you, O Lord, well know" (Psalm 40:9 NLT). Then he goes on to say, "I have not kept the good news of your justice hidden in my heart; I have talked about your faithfulness and saving power. I have told everyone in the great assembly of your unfailing love and faithfulness" (Psalm 40:10 NLT).

David knew first-hand what it was like to have God intervene in his life and rescue him from trouble, forgive him of sin, provide him with victory, heal him from sickness, and restore him to a right relationship with Himself. David knew that a relationship with God was not all about doing things for Him in order to keep Him satisfied or score brownie points with Him. "You take no delight in sacrifices or offerings" David told God (Psalm 40:6 NLT). No, God wants His followers to take joy in doing His will because they have experienced His faithful, unconditional love. They want to express their gratitude through obedience and submission to His will for their lives – because they know He loves them and has their best interests at heart. In fact, David said about God, "Your plans for us are too numerous to list. You have no equal. If I tried to recite all your wonderful deeds, I would never come to the end of them" (Psalm 40:5 NLT). David had a lot to say about God because God was an active and vital part of his life. Can the same thing be said of us? If we tried to recite all the wonderful things He has done for us lately, would we run out of time before we ran out of list? David called on God because he expected God to act. David waited on God because he was confident God would respond. David told others about God because he had plenty of stories of God's faithfulness to tell. He said, "May those who love your salvation repeatedly shout, 'The Lord is great!'" (Psalm 40:16b NLT). Maybe we have little to say about God because we so seldom turn to God for help and place on Him all our hope. "Oh, the joys of those who trust in the Lord" (Psalm 40:4a NLT).

Father, the problem is not that You are silent in my life, it is that I don't recognize and appreciate Your activity. I don't see it, so I don't acknowledge it. You are working all the time on my behalf, but I tend to be blind to it. I also don't turn to You enough in times of trouble and trust You for deliverance. I try to solve all my own problems. In doing so, I rob You of glory and deny myself the opportunity to see Your power on display in my life. I want to be a greater witness for You by being more satisfied by You. I want to sing Your praises more and tell everyone I meet of all Your wonderful acts. Amen

PSALM 40 – DAY 2

Something Worth Talking About.
Based on Psalm 40

I expectantly waited on God,
And hearing my cry for help, He turned toward me.
He brought me up out of dark place,
Where I was stuck, and unable to free myself.
But He put me back on solid ground,
And gave me a firm path for my feet.
He put a new song in my mouth,
A song of thanksgiving to our God.
For many who hear it, it will result in a reverence for God,
Causing them to trust Him more.

Happy is the man who refuses to follow the way of the proud,
Or turns aside to believe their lies,
But instead puts his trust in God.
All the wonderful things You've done for us God are too great to count,
I couldn't even begin to tell about all the plans You have arranged for us,

Sacrifices and offerings are not what You want from us.
I can hear You clearly now,
And burnt offerings and sin offerings are not what You are asking for.
Then I said, "I come before You because of what is written in Your word,
I find joy in doing what You want me to do,
Because Your law is written on my heart.

I have talked about Your righteousness to large crowds,
And You know I didn't hold anything back, Lord.
I didn't keep what I know of Your righteousness to myself,
But I have openly talked about Your faithfulness and salvation.
I didn't try to hide news of Your mercy and truth from anyone.

So I ask You not to withhold Your compassion from me, Lord.
Let Your mercy and truth continually guard and preserve me,
Because I find myself surrounded by all kinds of bad things,
The guilt of my sins has overtaken me,
So that I can't even see clearly anymore.
The number of my sins seems greater than the hairs on my head,
And I have lost all hope.

I beg You Lord to find it in Your heart to save me.
I need You to hurry up and help me.
Let those who would want to harm me be sorely disappointed.
Let those who wish me ill-will be turned aside in humiliation.
Let their shouts of joy over my demise be turned to devastation.

But let all of us who seek our security in You find joy and gladness.
May all of us who love Your salvation be able to say repeatedly,
"The Lord is great!"
Yet here I am, poor and needy, and the Lord takes notice of me,
He is my help and source of deliverance.
So don't hesitate for a second Lord! Act now!

PSALM 40 – DAY 3

Write Psalm 40 in your own words or write a psalm of your own. Be honest and open. Don't be afraid to tell God how you feel, but also include praise for who He is and all that He has done and is going to do in your life.

PSALM 41 – DAY 1

Lifting Up Those Who Are Down.

Oh, the joys of those who are kind to the poor! The Lord rescues them when they are in trouble. – Psalm 41:1 NLT

At first glance, this Psalm seems a bit disjointed. He starts out talking about the poor and how God blesses those who show them kindness. The next thing David is confessing his sin and crying out for mercy because of the apparent consequences of that sin. His problem seems to have nothing to do with poverty or need, but is due to his own willful sin. But if you look closer at the word translated "poor" in verse one, you find out that it can also be translated "one who is low or weak." It is from a root word that means "something hanging low."[10] It refers to something or someone languishing, being weak or powerless. So David is not necessarily talking about poverty as it relates to finances, but he is talking about spiritual and emotional poverty, and he is speaking from experience.

David is suffering because of sin. He has confessed that sin to God, but he is still experiencing the consequences of whatever it is he has done. He has close acquaintances who come to visit him in his pain and suffering, but who gossip about him when they leave and wish him nothing but ill-will. They look at his condition and, rather than encourage him, they try to figure out what it is wrong with him, what he has done to deserve something so bad, and debate when he is going to die. David knows he has done nothing to deserve this kind of treatment from his friends. If you recall, back in Psalm 35, David said that when his enemies were sick, he grieved for them. He even prayed and fasted for them, feeling sadness for their condition, "as though they were my friends or family" (Psalm 35:14 NLT). But now that David is down and out, his "friends" have become his enemies. So David is left to seek mercy from God.

---

[10] "H1800 - dal – Strong's Hebrew Lexicon (KJV)." Blue Letter Bible. Web. 9 Aug, 2016. https://www.blueletterbible.org

But what a reminder to those of us who claim to be Christ-followers that we are to have the same heart He had. We are to love like He loved. Jesus said of Himself, "The Spirit of the Lord is upon me, for he has anointed me to bring Good News to the poor. He has sent me to proclaim that captives will be released, that the blind will see, that the oppressed will be set free, and that the time of the Lord's favor has come" (Luke 4:18-19 NLT). We are to carry on that ministry to the down and out today. The Proverbs of Solomon remind us that our words carry weight. They are powerful and can accomplish good or bring about evil in the lives of others. "The words of the godly are a life-giving fountain" (Proverbs 10:11). "The words of the godly encourage many" (Proverbs 10:21). Solomon also warns that "with their words, the godless destroy their friends" (Proverbs 11:9). "Some people make cutting remarks, but the words of the wise bring healing" (Proverbs 12:18).

We are the hands, the feet, and the mouthpieces for Christ here on this earth. We are to have a heart for the lowly and all those who are languishing, whether it is because of their own sin or the sinful condition of the world in which we live. There are those who are languishing in financial poverty, but there are also those who are suffering in emotional and spiritual poverty. We are to bring them words of encouragement and healing. We are to show them mercy and grace. We are to love them with both words and actions. David knew that to do so was a rewarding experience. To do so was to live a life that was pleasing to God. God rewards those who care for and encourage the down and out. He repays them in kind. He "rescues them when they are in trouble" (Psalm 41:1 NLT).

Father, give me a heart for the down and out. Help me to see them all around me. It is easy to see the financially poor, but the spiritually and emotionally impoverished are all around me and they tend to hide their condition well. Don't let me be like David's friends, who because of their treatment of him in his time of need, were no better than enemies to him. May I be a true friend to those in need, providing words of encouragement and actions that back up what I say. Amen

PSALM 41 – DAY 2

Have Mercy!
Based on Psalm 41

Happy is the man who carefully considers the weak and powerless.
God delivers them in the midst of their bad times.
He continually watches over them and sustains their lives.
He leads them in the right way to go as they walk this earth,
And refuses to deliver them over to their enemies.
He comforts them when they are sick in bed,
And returns them to health.

That's why I prayed, "Have mercy on me.
Heal my soul, cleanse me from sin."
I am surrounded by those who say malicious things about me.
They ask, "When will God destroy him and destroy his reputation?"
If they come to see me, anything they say to me is worthless,
Their hearts are full of worthless thoughts about me,
And when they leave my presence, they share them with others.
They secretly judge me and assume the worst about me.
"His situation is due to wickedness," they say.
"He'll never recover from this one."
Even the man I considered my friend, the one I trusted,
And shared life with, has turned on me.

So Lord, I ask You to show me mercy,
Lift me up, restore me, and that will put an end to them.
This will let me know that You take delight in me,
Because You won't allow them to shout in victory over me.
You keep me whole and complete, allowing me to stand in Your presence,
I bless and adore You Lord, the God of Israel, forever and ever. Amen and Amen.

PSALM 41 – DAY 3

Write Psalm 41 in your own words or write a psalm of your own. Be honest and open. Don't be afraid to tell God how you feel, but also include praise for who He is and all that He has done and is going to do in your life.

PSALM 51 – DAY 1

Grace That Is Greater.

Purify me from my sins, and I will be clean; wash me, and I will be whiter than snow. Oh, give me back my joy again; you have broken me – now let me rejoice. – Psalm 51:7-8 NLT

> *Marvelous grace of our loving Lord,*
> *Grace that exceeds our sin and our guilt!*
> *Yonder on Calvary's mount out-poured,*
> *There where the blood of the Lamb was spilled.*
>
> *Grace, grace, God's grace,*
> *Grace that will pardon and cleanse within;*
> *Grace, grace, God's grace,*
> *Grace that is greater than all our sin.*[11]

Grace that is greater than all our sin. What a marvelous, almost impossible truth for us to comprehend. That God could love us so much that He would be willing to extend us grace in spite of our consistent struggle with sin. David knew this truth first-hand. Here in Psalm 51 we have the aftermath of his sin with Bathsheba. Here is the man known as the man after God's own heart, the king of Israel, wrestling with the guilt and conviction of his affair with this woman and his premeditated murder of her husband in order that he might have her as his own. This is a sin of the first degree. It is something that shocks even the most hard-core agnostic or atheist. These kinds of things are just not done in civilized society. But here is the leader of God's chosen people confessing his guilt and willingly accepting God just judgment. "Against you, and you alone, have I sinned; I have done what is evil in your sight. You will be proved right in what you say, and your judgment against me is just" (Psalm 51:4 NLT).

---

[11] Johnson, Julie H., Hymns Tried and True (Chicago, Illinois: The Bible Institute Colportage Association, 1911), number 2

David knew he was guilty, but he also knew that God was ready and willing to forgive his sin and restore him to a right relationship with Himself. David also knew that God was the only one who *could* restore him. So he cries out to God for mercy. He appeals to God's unfailing love. He asks God to show him compassion. He begs God to blot our the stain of his sin, wash him clean from his guilt, and purify him from his sin. He knows only God can make him clean. Only God can restore his joy. Only God can give him a new heart. Only God can give him back the joy associated with salvation. Only God can give him the ability to obey. The key to David's appeal to God was his understanding that God was looking for true repentance that comes from a heart that is grieved over its treatment of His will as revealed in His Word. David knew that his sin was ultimately against God, not Bathsheba or Uriah, her husband. And David knew that God was looking for godly sorrow in his heart. Paul refers to this kind of sorrow in his letter to the Corinthian church. "For the kind of sorrow God wants us to experience leads us away from sin and results in salvation. There's no regret for that kind of sorrow. But worldly sorrow, which lacks repentance, results in spiritual death" (1 Corinthians 7:9-10 NLT).

The sacrifice God wanted from David had little to do with lambs and goats, blood or offerings. But it had everything to do with a broken and contrite heart. A heart that is broken and crushed because it understands that it has offended a holy, yet loving and merciful God. God wanted sacrifices offered in the right spirit, with the right kind of heart behind them. David's sin was against God and that sin needed to bother him as much as it did God. And it did. So David came to God in sorrow, repentance, openness, honesty, and complete reliance on God to restore him, and he had every confidence that He would – because David's God is a gracious, kind, loving, and merciful God. David's God was a forgiving God. His grace was greater than all of David's sins – from the smallest to the biggest. David's sins of adultery and murder rank high on our list of potential transgressions against God, and yet God was willing to extend mercy, grace and forgiveness even for these two heinous sins against His holiness. God's grace really is greater than all our sins. Grace, grace, God's grace, grace that will pardon and cleanse within; grace, grace, God's grace, grace that is greater than all our sin.

Father, thank You that Your grace truly is greater than my sin. And because of Your grace I can receive forgiveness, cleansing, complete restoration, joy and the constant awareness of Your love. Amen

PSALM 51 – DAY 2

What I Do And What God Does.
Based on Psalm 51

As a result of what I know about your inexhaustible love,
I ask you to be gracious to me and show me favor, Lord.
Because of what I know about your abundant mercy,
I ask you to wipe out all traces of my sin against You.
I need You to wash away my depravity repeatedly and thoroughly,
And cleanse me completely from my sinfulness.
I can't escape the disturbing realization that I am in rebellion against You.
Yes, it's You and You alone against whom I have sinned,
And my evil actions have been done right in front of Your face.
You've seen it all, so You have every right to speak up,
And any judgment you pronounce against me will be just.
I've been a sinner since the day I was born.
In fact, my sinful condition started at the point of conception.
Everyone needs to recognize that it's truth and faithfulness You desire,
And it's in the inner recesses of a man's life that you look for them.
It's in that place where no one else can see that You make Your wisdom known.

I need You to purify me from my sin so that I can be truly clean.
I need You to wash me so that the darkness of my sin becomes whiter than white.
Let me experience the joy and gladness that come with forgiveness.
Make me like a man whose bones were all broken, but is now able to dance!
Turn away from looking at my sins,
Wipe out the very memory of them.
Shape within me a new heart,
And give me a new spirit that is ready to serve You.
Don't let my sin expel me from Your presence,
And don't remove the presence of Your Spirit from my life.

Let me experience the joy again that comes with Your salvation,
And give me the capacity to willingly and gladly obey You.
Then my life will be an open lesson for other sinners to learn the life You recommend.

As a result, they will return to You as well.
Strip off the blood that stains me, O God of my salvation,
And I will sing the praises of Your righteousness.
Give me a reason to open my mouth and shout Your praises!

It's not the sacrifices I make for You that bring You pleasure, Lord.
Those are not the things that please You, or else that's what I would give You.
The kind of sacrifice You want begins with a broken spirit.
You won't look down on a heart that's truly broken and crushed.
Make Your people Your delight and do good to them,
Restore them.
Then the sacrifices they make will please You because they will be righteous,
Everything they do will bring you pleasure and joy.

PSALM 51 – DAY 3

Write Psalm 51 in your own words or write a psalm of your own. Be honest and open. Don't be afraid to tell God how you feel, but also include praise for who He is and all that He has done and is going to do in your life.

PSALM 52 – DAY 1

Good By God's Standards.

Look what happens to mighty warriors who do not trust in God. They trust their wealth instead and grow more and more bold in their wickedness. – Psalm 52:7 NLT

Doeg the Edomite had done a good thing. At least he thought so. He had done exactly what the king of Israel had commanded him to do and he knew it was going to win him favor in the king's eyes. The fact that he had personally killed 85 priests of God along with all their family members didn't seem to bother him. The fact that the members of King Saul's personal bodyguard had each refused to kill the Lord's priests didn't seem to concern him either. When King Saul turned to Doeg and presented him with the opportunity to prove his loyalty, he stepped up to the challenge. It all began when David was forced to run away from Saul in order to preserve his life. King Saul was out to kill him, because he was jealous of David's fame and feared that he was going to take his place as king of Israel. He had already tried to kill David with his own hands, so David was forced to run for his life. One of the first places David went was to the town of Nob to see Ahimelech the priest. Ahimelech gave David food and the sword of Goliath, which had been kept there ever since David had killed the Philistine champion in battle. Little did David know that Doeg the Edomite, one of King Saul's chief herdsmen, was there in Nob and saw the whole exchange between David and Ahimelech. He went back to Saul and reported that the priest had aided and abetted David, a fugitive from justice.

As a result of Doeg's news, King Saul commanded the slaughter of all 85 of the priests of God living in Nob, along with their families. When Saul's bodyguard refused to do Saul's bidding, Doeg, the herdsmen, was given a chance to improve his station in life by proving his loyalty and displaying his bravery to the king. And evidently, according to David, Doeg the Edomite even bragged about his brave "exploits" against the unarmed priests of God, trying to present himself as a mighty warrior. He had a knack for blowing the whole affair out of proportion, expanding the story with fanciful lies designed to justify his actions and boost his fame. David accused him of being "an expert at telling lies" (Psalm 52:3 NLT). David saw Doeg for what he really was: a man who loved evil more than good. He was a man who tried to distort reality by making evil appear as if it was good. At the end of the day, Doeg the Edomite cared more about himself than he did about God. He didn't fear God or desire to do the will of God. He was obsessed with his own well-being and self-gratification. No doubt Saul rewarded him well for his "brave" handling of the whole affair.

While David was a man after God's own heart (1 Samuel 13:14), Doeg was a man after Saul's own heart. Like Saul, he wasn't interested in doing what God wanted done. He was a selfish, self-centered man who longed to make a name for himself. His destruction of God's priests was probably well rewarded by Saul. More than likely, he was raised from chief herdsman to warrior status. He got a promotion out of the whole thing, more than likely, a raise, and the praise of the king. But David warned Doeg about the reality of his situation. God was going to repay Doeg in full for what he had done. David says, "Look what happens to mighty warriors who do not trust in God. They trust their wealth instead and grow more and more bold in their wickedness" (Psalm 52:7 NLT). David sarcastically refers to Doeg as a "mighty warrior" and accuses him of trusting his new-found wealth instead of God. He had become addicted to his fame and fortune and become increasingly more wicked, looking for additional opportunities to pad his resume and expand his wealth.

But those who do "good" that is not based on God's standards will never win in the end. They may receive rewards and recognition in this life, but they will always get what they really deserve when all is said and done. David preferred to trust in God. Rather than take matters into his own hands and do what appeared to be good by worldly standards, he would do only what God would have him do. On two different occasions, David had the opportunity to murder King Saul, and had he done so, he could have put an end to his fugitive lifestyle. Even David's companions encouraged him to kill Saul, viewing it as a God-provided opportunity to rid himself of Saul once and for all. But David refused, knowing that God had not given him permission to kill the king. He knew that God would take care of King Saul in His own time and according to His own terms. David would simply trust God. And God came through. Eventually, God eliminated Saul and elevated David to the throne. David trusted and God provided. Which is why David could say, "I am like an olive tree, thriving in the house of God. I will always trust in God's unfailing love. I will praise you forever, O God, for what you have done. I will trust in your good name in the presence of your faithful people" (Psalm 52:8-9 NLT).

Doeg trusted in himself. David trusted in God. Doeg was out for himself. David was out for God. Doeg looked successful, but would eventually fail. At one time David appeared abandoned by God and was an apparent failure in the world's eyes. But He trusted God and was rewarded by Him for his faithfulness. David did good according to God's standards and enjoyed true success. Doeg did good according to the world's standards and failed in the end. We aren't told what happened to Doeg the Edomite, but we can rest assured that God repaid him in full for what he had done – either in this life or in the next. David knew that God would deal with Doeg justly. "But God will strike you down once and for all. He will pull you from your home and uproot you from the land of the living" (Psalm 52:5 NLT). David trusted God.

Father, this world is constantly tempting us to live according to its standards. It wants us to do good on its terms, but You call us to trust You and to live according to Your standards. Keep reminding us Lord that Your way is the not only the best way, it is the only way. Your will trumps our will every time. Doing what is right in our own eyes or according to the world's standards is never a profitable path to take. Amen

PSALM 52 – DAY 2

Misplaced Trust.
Based on Psalm 52

Why do you boast about all the wrong you've done, oh "mighty man"?
God's mercy and love will outlast you.
Your tongue is like a sharp razor, planning evil and working deception.
You love evil more than good and prefer telling lies instead of the truth.

You love to destroy others with your words and destructive lies.
But God has everlasting destruction planned for you,
He is going to grab you and rip you right out of your comfortable home,
He will pull you up by the roots – removing your life altogether.

Those who are righteous in conduct and character will watch it happen,
They will be in awe of God and laugh at you.
"Look how this 'mighty man' refused to find his strength in God,
Instead he sought safety in the abundance of his wealth,
And grew confident and strong through his pursuit of evil."

But as for me, I am like a flourishing olive tree in God's house.
I have permanently put my trust in His love and mercy.
I will continually give thanks to Him for He has made it possible.
I will expectantly wait on Him, based on His reputation,
For His people have found Him to be good all the time.

PSALM 52 – DAY 3

Write Psalm 52 in your own words or write a psalm of your own. Be honest and open. Don't be afraid to tell God how you feel, but also include praise for who He is and all that He has done and is going to do in your life.

PSALMS 53-54 – DAY 1

Bad Times. Good God.

God looks down from heaven on the entire human race; he looks to see if anyone is truly wise, if anyone seeks God. But no, all have turned away; all have become corrupt. No one does good, not a single one! – Psalm 53:2-3 NLT

According to God, the world is full of fools – those individuals who act and live as if there is no God. Even those who claim to know Him act as if He either doesn't care about what they do or He is too powerless to do anything about it. Then there are those who just refuse to believe in Him altogether. These people "are corrupt, and their actions are evil; not one of them does good!" (Psalm 53:1 NLT). This is not a very promising assessment on the character or condition of mankind. It leaves little doubt, at least from God's perspective, that man is inherently wicked and in open rebellion against Him. Yet God is still reaching out to man, offering mercy and forgiveness. He will ultimately be forced to punish all those who refuse to accept His offer of new life through His Son; but until then, He keeps providing opportunities for them to repent and return to Him.

And while the world is a less-than-ideal place, full of people obsessed with their own agendas, consumed by their own importance, and controlled by their own sin natures, David gives us a glimpse of God's goodness as he reminds us that God is always there for us even in the midst of all the evil that surrounds us. "But God is my helper. The Lord keeps me alive!" (Psalm 54:4 NLT). David appeals to God's power and places himself at God's mercy to rescue him from his enemies. Those who care nothing at all for God are making David's life miserable. But David knows he can call out to God, and not only will God hear him, He will answer. David has seen the goodness of God time and time again in his life, delivering him from troubles and trials, rescuing him from every conceivable kind of predicament. And while he is a firm believer that "no one does good, not a single one," David knows that God can and does do good for those who love Him. And David's response is to offer God praise and gratitude. He says, "I will sacrifice a voluntary offering to you" – not something required or coerced, but of his own free will. "I will praise your name, O Lord, for it is good" (Psalm 54:6 NLT). God's name, which is really a reference to His reputation or fame, is nothing but good. All that God does is good, even when He has to deal with those who are bad. God is righteous, always doing what is the right thing to do. He never does wrong. He is just in all His actions towards men. He never punishes unjustly or unfairly. He is good. And it doesn't matter whether men reject Him, ignore Him, or attempt to deny He even exists. God remains good even when things appear bad.

Father, we live in a world that is sick and dying. It is filled with people who refuse to love and serve You. Many refuse to even believe in You. And yet, You remain good. You continue to make the sun shine on all men, showering them with Your common grace. You make the crops grow, the rain to fall, and the air breathable. You constantly offer the free gift of grace available through Your Son. And You care for Your own, providing them with a listening ear and a powerful hand to rescue and restore them. You are indeed a good God. Amen

PSALMS 53-54 – DAY 2

The Heart Of A Fool.
Based on Psalm 53

It takes a real fool to try and convince themselves,
"There is no God!"
Which is why they end up all twisted, doing nothing but evil,
And never doing anything that is good in God's eyes.

It's like God is looking down on men from His place in heaven,
In an attempt to see if anybody gets it, if anybody has a desire to seek Him.
But they've all left Him long ago.
Every one of them is corrupt morally and spiritually.
Not a single, solitary one of them does what God considers good.

These people act unconcerned, consuming God's people as flippantly as eating bread.
"Is it that they don't know Me that they refuse to call on Me?," God asks.
They don't fear God now, but one day they will.
God will one day destroy them all, leaving them completely disappointed,
Because He will reject them in the end.

But I long for salvation to come from the Lord.
I look forward to the day when He restores His people.
When He does, everyone, including me, will shout with joy.

The Hope Of A Believer
Based on Psalm 54

Save me God, in keeping with Your righteous reputation.
Use Your incredible power to vindicate me.
Hear me when I pray to You,
Listen to what I have to say.
People I don't even know have taken a stand against me,
Terrible people are out for my life.
These are people who have no place for God in their lives.

But You are my helper,
And You show up through those who support me.
You'll pay back my enemies, giving them what they deserve,
Which is why I worship You freely and gladly.
I praise You because Your good reputation has been proven in my life.
You have always provided a way out of all my troubles,
And allowed me to view my enemies from Your perspective.

PSALMS 53-54 – DAY 3

Write Psalm 53 in your own words or write a psalm of your own. Be honest and open. Don't be afraid to tell God how you feel, but also include praise for who He is and all that He has done and is going to do in your life.

PSALMS 53-54 – DAY 3

Write Psalm 54 in your own words or write a psalm of your own. Be honest and open. Don't be afraid to tell God how you feel, but also include praise for who He is and all that He has done and is going to do in your life.

PSALM 55 – DAY 2

Don't Run Away. Run To God.

Give your burdens to the Lord, and he will take care of you. He will not permit the godly to slip and fall. – Psalm 55:22 NLT

My wife has a phrase she tends to use when things are not going well. She'll say, "I wish we could go to an island." When those words come out of her mouth, she is expressing the same thing David did when he said, "Oh, that I had wings like a dove; then I would fly away and rest! I would fly far away to the quiet of the wilderness. How quickly I would escape – far from this wild storm of hatred" (Psalm 55:6-8 NLT). Both David and my wife occasionally find themselves in situations that cause them to want to run away and hide. My wife pictures a secluded island, far from the cares and troubles that confront us. For David, it was the wilderness of Judea, outside the walls of Jerusalem. Which I find interesting, because that same wilderness is where David spent so many years hiding from the paid assassins of King Saul who were on a mission to take his life. You would think that the wilderness would be the last place David would want to go, but those barren, rocky hills had become a place of refuge, peace, and protection for him. It was in the wilderness that he found rest, safety, and a sense of well-being. Life as the king living within the crowded walls of Jerusalem was anything but easy. There was intrigue, infighting, money issues, family quarrels, government concerns, and the constant threat of war because of all of Israel's enemies. Then there was the pressure of being king and shepherd over the people of God. David was under a tremendous amount of pressure. On top of that, he had had one of his closest friends turn on him. David says, "It is not an enemy who taunts me – I could bear that. It is not my foes who so arrogantly insult me – I could have hidden from them. Instead, it is you – my equal, my companion and close friend" (Psalm 55:12-13 NLT). We aren't told what happened between David and this unnamed individual, but it must have been bad. It is so bad that David wants to run away and hide. Much like he did when his son, Absalom, stole the hearts of the people. Rather than face his son and protect his throne, David ran away. And now he was tempted to do so again. Running is always an attractive option. Some of us run away from problems literally, while others of us do it mentally and emotionally. We may run to busyness, drowning our problems through preoccupation with something else. We may run to drugs or alcohol, attempting to cloud our perception that the problem even exists. We may run to some form of entertainment, hoping to distract our minds from the issue at hand. Or we may run from our problems by attempting to ignore them altogether. But whatever tactic we take, running from our problems rarely ever works, and it never really makes them go away. David knew that.

So instead of running or flying away, David ran to God. He called to God and asked Him to do what only God can do – provide rescue and relief. David knew from experience that "God, who has ruled forever, will hear me and humble them" (Psalm 55:19 NLT). As bad as things might have been, David knew that God was fully capable of handling his problems, his enemies, his clash with his former friend, and anything else that came up in his life. His advice? "Give your burdens to the Lord, and he will take care of you. He will not permit the godly to slip and fall" (Psalm 55:22 NLT). Running away may provide distance from our problems, but it can never provide resolution. Only God can do that. We can confidently face whatever comes our way by taking it to the Lord and turning it over to Him. Don't run away. Run to Him. He is where we will find peace, safety, rescue, and resolution to our problems.

Father, I am not sure why I don't run to You more often and more readily. You have never failed me or let me down in the least, but I still find myself running away rather than running to You. When faced with problems, I long for escape, when what I should long for is You. You alone can help me. You alone can rescue me. You alone are the answer to every problem that confronts me. Amen

PSALM 55 – DAY 2

A Friend In Deed.
Based on Psalm 55

Hear me when I pray, O God.
Don't disappear when I cry to You for help!
Listen closely and answer quickly.
I wander around in a state of anxiety, disturbed and distracted,
All because of what my enemies say about me,
And the pressure put on me by the ungodly.
They rock my world with misfortune,
And attack me out of anger.
My heart aches within me and I fear for my life.
I'm so scared I shake.
In fact, my whole body shudders.
So I end up screaming, "If only I could fly like a dove,
Then I could escape and find a place to rest."
I would hurry up and get away from all the storms of life.
Confuse their words and make what they say impossible to understand,
For I see that it all produces violence and contention.
They act like a guard patrolling the walls of a city,
While nothing but trouble takes place inside.
The whole place is filled with evil desire,
Oppression and deceit are found on every street.
But in my case, it wasn't an enemy who ended up scorning me.
I could have handled that.
It wasn't someone who hated me and tried to oppress me.
If that was the case, I could have just hidden from him.
But no, it was you, a close friend and acquaintance,
Someone just like me.
We shared a close, intimate relationship,
And even enjoyed a mutual love for God.
As for the others, may their lives end in death,
May their actions end them up in hell,
Because their entire lives are filled with evil.

But as for me, I will call on God,
And He will save me.
I will pray from morning to evening,
And He will hear my voice.
It doesn't matter how many are against me,
Because God will deliver my life from the battle.
The very God who has reigned for eternity will hear me and put them to shame.
Their lives never change because they have no fear of God.
Even my former friend breaks his promises and turns on me.
He said all the right things, but all the while he was out to harm me.
His words were slick, covering up his real intention — my destruction.

But you can roll all your burdens onto the Lord,
And He will sustain you.
He will never let down those who are godly.
But God will bring about the destruction of the ungodly.
Their lives will come to a quick end,
They will end up with half the normal life expectancy.
But I will trust in You, God.

PSALM 55 – DAY 3

Write Psalm 55 in your own words or write a psalm of your own. Be honest and open. Don't be afraid to tell God how you feel, but also include praise for who He is and all that He has done and is going to do in your life.

PSALM 56 – DAY 1

Nobody Knows The Trouble I've Seen.

You keep track of all my sorrows. You have collected all my tears in your bottle. You have recorded each one in your book. – Psalm 56:8 NLT

> *Sometimes I'm up*
> *And sometimes I'm down*
> *Yes, Lord, you know sometimes I'm almost to the ground*
> *Oh, yes, Lord, still*
> *Nobody knows the trouble I've seen*
> *Nobody knows but Jesus*
> *Nobody knows the trouble I've seen*
> *Glory, Hallelujah*[12]

While those familiar lyrics were made famous by Louis Armstrong, they could be the anthem of every believer who has ever lived. We all face troubles of all kinds. Some are physical, others financial. Some of our troubles are self-induced, while others come at us unexpectedly and undeservedly. Some of are short-term, while others hang around us for years at a time, even for our a lifetime. But as the lyrics state so well, even when everybody else is oblivious to our troubles, Jesus knows. He is well aware of every circumstance going on in our lives. David found comfort in his troubles because he knew that God knew. He said, "God is on my side" (Psalm 56:9 NLT) and he believed it. In the midst of trouble, David put his hope and trust in the Lord. "I trust in God, so why should I be afraid? What can mere mortals do to me?" (Psalm 56:11 NLT). But before we place David on a pedestal and elevate him to sainthood, let's remind ourselves that this psalm was written *after* he ran away from King Saul and fled to his arch enemies, the Philistines, for protection. That's not exactly trusting in God, is it? He didn't run to God, he ran to King Achish. At every level this does not appear to be a bright move on David's part. Early

---

[12] Armstrong, Louis. "Nobody Knows The Trouble I've Seen". Brunswick. 1966.
http://www.songlyrics.com

in his career David had made a name for himself by killing the Philistine champion, Goliath, in a one-on-one battle. The Philistines had never forgotten or forgiven David. On top of that, since his defeat of Goliath, David had built a reputation for being a mighty warrior. In fact, there was already a song about David with lyrics that said, "Saul has killed his thousands, and David his ten thousands!" (1 Samuel 18:7 NLT). And many of those David had slain were Philistines. So why on earth did David run to the Philistines for protection? We're not told, but we can guess that David hoped they would see him as some kind of secret weapon and when they discovered he and King Saul were at odds, they would assume they could use him against the Israelites. But when David arrived in the Philistine territory, the reception he found a less-than-welcoming reception. They immediately recognized him and were ready to kill him. So David was forced to feign insanity, and had to act like he had completely lost his mind. Even the blood thirsty Philistines were unwilling to kill a lunatic, so they allowed him to leave.

It was after David got out of this sticky situation that he wrote, "you have rescued me from death; you have kept my feet from slipping" (Psalm 56:13 NLT). David realized, after the fact, that God had protected him even when he had refused to turn to God for protection. It wasn't his great acting ability that had saved his life, but God. David had learned a valuable lesson: "But when I am afraid, I will put my trust in you" (Psalm 56:3 NLT). Troubles were going to come. Trials were just around the corner. David was always going to have somewhat like Saul in his life. But he had learned that he could trust God. God knew his troubles, and God had a solution. David didn't have to fear Saul, Achish, the Philistines or any other man. He simply had to trust the promises of God.

Father, sometimes I'm up and sometimes I'm down, but You are always right there with me, fully aware of my situation and ready to take care of me in the midst of them. You know what is going on. You are aware and I can trust You to help me at all times. Amen

PSALM 56 – DAY 2

Learning To Trust God By Failing To Trust God.
Based on Psalm 56

Graciously extend Your favor to me, O God,
For it seems like everybody is so busy trying to destroy me, they're out of breath.
Every day it's like they're fighting to squeeze the life out of me.
Their attempts to crush me are a daily occurrence,
And their numbers seem to be increasing.
But when those times come that cause me to fear,
I will put my trust and confidence in You.
I will end up offering praise to You because of all Your promises to me.
In the past I have learned to put my trust and confidence in You,
So why in the world would I fear anything that men might do to me in the future?

At those times, they try to influence what I say by what they do,
Planning nothing but evil to do to me.
They hide their intent to harm me,
watching my every move, waiting for a chance to destroy my soul.
Are they going to get away with all the trouble they cause me?
Let them see the anger on Your face firsthand, O God,
Cut them down to size!

You have an accurate count of every time I aimlessly wandered,
And You've recorded them on Your ledger.
You've also collected the tears I cried at those moments in a bottle.

And I know that the next time I have to cry out to You,
You'll turn my enemies back, because You're my God!
I will end up praising You because You are God and You always come through,
You are Jehovah and You always do what You say You'll do.
I have put my confidence and trust in You before, God,
So there's no reason I should fear what man might do to me now.

You've always kept Your promises, God,
So I will repay You with praises!
On more than one occasion You have snatched my life from the brink of death,
Keeping me from falling and allowing me to live life on this side of the grave!

PSALM 56 – DAY 3

Write Psalm 56 in your own words or write a psalm of your own. Be honest and open. Don't be afraid to tell God how you feel, but also include praise for who He is and all that He has done and is going to do in your life.

PSALM 57 – DAY 1

A Heart For God.

My heart is confident in you, O God; my heart is confident. No wonder I can sing your praises! – Psalm 57:7 NLT

David is hiding out in a cave in the middle of the wilderness. He is running from crazy King Saul who has set a bounty on his head, and is out to see David's memory wiped from the face of the earth. In looking back at his circumstances, David crafts a song to tell others what he has learned about his God through the midst of it all. He pens the lyrics to a hymn of praise that chronicles the goodness of God in the midst of the difficulties of life. David is being chased. He is being hounded. His very life is in danger. He is surrounded by enemies and facing unbelievable opposition. Yet he has been anointed king by the prophet, Samuel, and appointed by God Himself to be the next king of Israel. So he calls out to God, asking Him to bring about what He has promised. "I cry out to God Most High, to God who will fulfill His purpose for me" (Psalm 57:2 NLT). All the way back at his anointing by Samuel, David had heard the Lord say, "This is the one; anoint him" (1 Samuel 16:12 NLT). Then Samuel had poured the oil onto David's head and God poured His Spirit into David's heart. In doing so, God was promising David that he would one day be the king of Israel. Yes, Saul was still on the throne and David was hiding out in a cave in the wilderness, but in spite of those circumstances, God was going to keep His promise. David was confident of that. In Psalm 56, written based on David's experience of fleeing from Saul and seeking refuge among the Philistines (a plan that didn't work out too well for him), David learned to trust in God's promise. He wrote, "This I know: God is on my side!" (Psalm 56:9 NLT).

David can sing God's praises because He had learned to trust God's promises. He didn't wait until God had completely fulfilled them all and he was on the throne of Israel. No, David sang God's praises from the depths of a cave in the middle of the wilderness, years before he ever put a crown on his head or set foot in the city of Jerusalem. David sang of God's love and faithfulness in anticipation of God's future fulfillment of His promises.

We can praise Him now for what He is going to do later, because God always comes through. He is good on His word. David cried out to God knowing that He would send help from heaven to rescue him. In due time, God would do what He had promised to do. And He still works the same way today. We can trust Him because He is trustworthy.

Father, may I be able to say, "My heart is confident in you, my heart is confident." And may I be able to say it long before You've proven it true. May I praise You based on Your reputation for faithfulness, not just because You've proven it. Amen

PSALM 57 – DAY 2

In A Cave, But Confident.
Based on Psalm 57

I ask You to show me favor, O God,
Please show me favor.
I have put my life in Your hands for protection,
Not in this cave in which I'm hiding.
All my hope, trust and confidence is in You.
And I will keep putting my hope, trust and confidence in You
Until You have caused all this trouble to pass me by.
I cry out to the Most High God!
To You, God, who alone can bring a fitting conclusion to the affairs of my life.
You simply have to say the word from heaven,
And I am saved from being plucked off by those who would destroy me,
From all who are out to crush me.
You speak and Your mercy and truth replace all the hatred and lies.
I feel like a man who is surrounded by hungry lions,
They are burning with the desire to consume me.
But they're really men with literal spears and arrows,
And whose words against me pierce like a sharp sword.
So I ask You to rise up, O God!
From Your place in the highest heavens,
Rise up and let Your glory fill the earth!
My path is surrounded by traps,
So that I have to walk bent over so that I don't fall into one of them.
They've even dug a pit just for me,
But instead they've fallen into it themselves!
My heart is ready for anything, O God,
My heart is ready for anything!
Which is why I can offer You praise even now.
I am excited!
I get up early and lift up Your praise in song!
I will praise You along with all those who believe in You,
But I will also praise in front of those who don't.

Your unfailing love knows no limits,
And Your faithfulness to me is boundless.
So I ask You to rise up, O God!
From Your place in the highest heavens,
Rise up and let Your glory fill the earth!

PSALM 57 – DAY 3

Write Psalm 57 in your own words or write a psalm of your own. Be honest and open. Don't be afraid to tell God how you feel, but also include praise for who He is and all that He has done and is going to do in your life.

PSALM 58 – DAY 1

Justice For The Unjust.

Then at last everyone will say, "There truly is a reward for those who live for God; surely there is a God who judges justly here on earth." – Psalm 58:11 NLT

There are times when injustice seems to be everywhere. We read the newspaper or watch TV and are appalled at what we find there. The innocent suffer at the hands of the wicked. The weak fall prey to the strong. Bigger nations take advantage of smaller ones. And nobody seems capable of doing anything about it. Governments posture and promote plans to bring about justice, but their efforts make little or no dent in the situation. Oftentimes, those very same governments are perpetrating acts of injustice of their own. As David put it, violence continues to spread through the land. Nobody seems to even know what justice really means anymore. Except God. Even though David felt as if justice was a lost cause in his day, he knew he could appeal to God because He is just and righteous. God not only sees all the injustice going on, He can do something about it. Even though David felt impotent to do anything about "these wicked people" who "spit venom like deadly snakes," he knew that God was more than powerful enough to deal with it all. So he turns to God. In his frustration, David asks God to do to these people exactly what he would do if he could. His request is graphic and less-than-compassionate. David pulls no punches. He asks God to wipe these people off the face of the earth. At first blush, a reading of David's request to God might disturb us. It comes across as so violent and unloving. But it also reveals David's hatred of injustice. He can't stand to see the unjust go unpunished, because he understands that they are in direct opposition to his God. He refuses to tolerate or grow accustomed to injustice, just because he is powerless to do anything about it. But too often we do just that. We grow callous about it all because there appears to be nothing we can do. We read the stories of injustice going on in the world and we turn a deaf ear and a blind eye. We tend to ignore what we feel like we can't impact. We know injustice is taking place, but because we feel powerless to do anything about it, we slowly learn to tolerate it – as long as it's not happening to us. But David was a man after God's own heart. He loved what God loved and hated what God hated. So David hated injustice and he appealed to the only one who could do anything about it. He asked God to act. He cried out to God to bring justice because God is just.

And here's what David was counting on: God will act. God will judge. God will bring justice. "Surely there is a God who judges justly here on the earth" (Psalm 58:11 NLT). The day is coming when justice really will prevail. God will deal with the unjust and avenge those who have suffered at their hands. When we see injustice taking place, we need to call out to God for His help. We need to ask Him what He would have us do as His hands and feet on this planet. Injustice should make us long for justice. Sin should make us long for His salvation. Wickedness should make us long for righteousness. Darkness should make us long for His light. Instead of ignoring injustice or becoming callous to its presence, we should learn to see it clearly and long to watch God remove it completely.

Father, there is injustice in the land. It is all around us and we are powerless to do anything about it. But You're not, so I ask that You intervene and that You do what only You can do. Bring justice. Protect the innocent. Establish righteousness. Remove wickedness. Send Your Son to right all wrong and avenge all injustice. So that the righteous might rejoice. Amen

PSALM 58 – DAY 2

Our Just God.
Based on Psalm 58

How can you people really talk about justice,
When it seems to be the last thing we hear in your judgments?
Do you judge fairly and rightly?
Far from it! Your decisions are driven by evil hearts.
You dispense violence rather than justice on the earth.
These people departed from truth and righteousness the minute they were born.
They wander from God's path at birth, speaking lies instead of truth.
The poison they spread is as deadly as that of a snake,
Incapable of listening to reason, they strike out with deadly accuracy.
They are like a cobra that the snake charmer can't control.
His wisdom and skills are wasted on them.

De-fang them, O God! Remove the power of their words.
Break off their teeth so they can't use their mouths to destroy others.
Let them disappear like raging waters that eventually run out.
Let them wither like grass that is here today and gone tomorrow.
May they go the way of the snail, that dries up when the heat comes.
Like a premature baby, may their lives be short-lived.
In the time it takes to light kindling under a cooking pot,
God will sweep them all away in His burning anger.

Those who are righteous and love justice will rejoice
When they see God enact vengeance on the unjust.
They will have to wade through the blood of the wicked when God is done.
The only conclusion anyone will be able to reach is,
"The life of righteousness bears fruit in the end,
Because God will eventually judge between the righteous and the wicked."

PSALM 58 – DAY 3

Write Psalm 58 in your own words or write a psalm of your own. Be honest and open. Don't be afraid to tell God how you feel, but also include praise for who He is and all that He has done and is going to do in your life.

PSALM 59 – DAY 1

Unchanging Love. Incomparable Power.

You are my strength; I wait for you to rescue me, for you, O God, are my fortress. In his unfailing love, my God will stand with me. He will let me look down in triumph on my enemies. – Psalm 59:9-10 NLT

I've had bad days, but I've never had someone who was out to kill me (at least that I know of). I've never been hunted down like a wild animal or had armed mercenaries lying in wait outside my home, just waiting for me to show up so they could take me out. But David had, and he wrote this psalm because of it. David knew what it meant to be hated, harassed, hounded, and hunted. He had experienced what it means to fear for your life. Every time he woke up he knew it would be another day filled with more of the same thing. But he also knew something that I too easily forget. He knew that God was with him, for him, and would rescue him – no matter what he faced that day. Which is why he could say, "But as for me, I will sing about your power. Each morning I will sing with joy about your unfailing love. For you have been my refuge, a place of safety when I am in distress" (Psalm 59:16 NLT). David had experienced the unfailing love of God on previous occasions, so he knew that he could trust God to show up no matter what he faced that day. David knew that God loved him and that love never failed. While his own friends had turned their backs on him, David's God was faithful and true. He would never let David down. "In his unfailing love, my God will stand with me" (Psalm 59:10 NLT).

But not only was God unfailing in his love and unwavering in His support for David, He was incomparable in power. In other words, God loved David, and that love was backed up by a strength that could protect David from anything and everything he faced. Love alone is not enough to prevent calamity from happening to someone who is dear to us. Many have had to watch helplessly as their loved ones died right before their eyes. Soldiers have had to watch, powerless to help, as their comrades died on the battlefield. Love for their brothers was strong, but incapable of preventing their deaths. But God's limitless love for us is backed by a power that is just as vast. He not only loves us, but is capable of protecting, rescuing, and saving us. His power to save us is motivated by His desire to save us. He rescues us because He loves us. He saves us not just because He can, but because His love demands it.

David knew about God's love because he had experienced God's love. But it was more than some kind of sentimental, sappy kind of love. It was love expressed in power, exhibited in strength, and proven in acts of divine intervention. David knew he was loved because he was still alive – in spite of all those who wanted him dead. His next breath was a reminder of God's love. Seeing the sun come up in the morning was an opportunity to thank God for His love and deliverance. David's problems still existed. His enemies were still there. But David knew that God would see him through the day, because God loved him, and that love was backed by power.

Father, how easy it is to forget that You love me – unceasingly. Somehow I know You are all powerful. But I sometimes doubt that You love me enough to make that power available to me each and every day. I fail to recognize that the very fact that I am alive is proof of Your power and Your love for me. Without Your sustaining power and unfailing love, I would cease to exist. You give me the strength I need to make it through the day. You lovingly sustain me, helping me make my way through the trials of life. May I learn to sing Your praises each and every morning, grateful for another day to serve You and watch You work in my life. Amen

PSALM 59 – DAY 2

Then The Whole World Will Know.
Based on Psalm 59

Snatch me out of trouble, O God.
Pull me right out of the middle of those who would destroy me.
Set me in a safe, hard-to-get-to place where they can't reach me.
Grab me away from those who do evil and shed blood.
They hide out, waiting to do me in.
They are strong and have it in for me,
Yet I have done nothing wrong to deserve this treatment.
They are in a hurry and determined to get me, in spite of my innocence.
So I turn to You, the God of all the armies of heaven.
I turn to You, the God of the armies of Israel.
Go into action, deal with the wicked and show no mercy.
They're like wild dogs, returning at night,
Snarling, growling, and prowling the streets in packs.
They can't keep down what they've eaten,
They spew forth all kinds of vile things,
Their words cut like a sharp sword.
They mock You, acting as if You can't hear what they're saying.
But You will have the last laugh, O God.
You will be the one doing the mocking in the end.
I will wait on You, because You have the power to do something about my situation.
You have the strength to defend me when others can't or won't.
Because of Your mercy, You will confront them,
You will allow me to stand over them in triumph.
I don't ask You to eliminate them completely,
Because then we would just forget we ever had a problem.
No, I ask You to knock them down a notch or two.
Deal with them because of the sin they commit with their words,
And because of the pride that is exposed by what comes out of their mouths.
They curse and lie constantly, so wipe them out completely!
Exterminate them completely in Your righteous anger.
Prove to them that You are on the throne and in complete control.

They're like wild dogs, returning at night,
Snarling, growling, and prowling the streets in packs,
But let them go to bed hungry and disappointed.
Let them wander in search of food, but all in vain.
But I am going to wake up singing Your praises!
I will sing about Your mercy in the morning,
For You have been like a fortress and a place of refuge,
Every time I have faced any kind of adversity.
You are my strength, so I sing Your praises
And thank You for Your unfailing love and constant protection.

PSALM 59 – DAY 3

Write Psalm 59 in your own words or write a psalm of your own. Be honest and open. Don't be afraid to tell God how you feel, but also include praise for who He is and all that He has done and is going to do in your life.

PSALM 60 – DAY 1

With God's Help.

"With God's help we will do mighty things, for he will trample down our foes." – Psalm 60:12 NLT

I can't imagine what it was like to have been king of the nation of Israel. While I'm sure the job had its perks, it also came with a significant number of headaches. Ruling any nation is difficult, but trying to lead a people group who happened to be the hand-picked possession of God Himself was no easy task. First, you had God for your employer. Forget about Congress, your cabinet, or even your constituents. At the end of the day, every action you took was being carefully critiqued by none other than God. Now that's pressure. On top of that you had the unenviable task of trying to lead a people who greatly disliked being led. Leading the nation of Israel was like, as the phrase goes, trying to herd cats – nearly impossible. By God's own opinion, these people were inherently stiff-necked, stubborn, rebellious, and had foreheads of iron. In other words, they were obstinate. And as the king of Israel you weren't free to make up your own rules as you went along. You were obligated to enforce the laws of God. Of course, some of Israel's kings ignored that part and suffered the consequences. But for David, obeying God was a high priority and maintaining His laws, decrees and commands was job one.

Then there was the problem of Israel's enemies, and there were a lot of them. This little land was literally surrounded on all sides by nations intent on their destruction – Philistines, Moabites, Ammonites, Aramaens, Edomites, Jebusites, and just about every other nation that existed at that time – both large and small. They all had it in for Israel and they were a constant threat to the nation's existence. As king, David had to be constantly prepared to defend the kingdom, as well as the reputation of God. And even though David was "a man after God's own heart," things didn't always go his way. He didn't always win every battle. His exploits didn't always meet with success. And this psalm was written with one of those times in mind. David opens up the psalm describing what had been an apparent defeat at the hands of his enemies. They had broken through his defenses. They had driven Israel back in defeat. And because David was so strongly dependent on God, he couldn't help but wonder if all this was some kind of punishment from His hand. He viewed this latest military setback as coming from God. So he appealed to God for mercy. He begged God to rescue the nation from the hands of their enemies. "Now rescue your beloved people. Answer and save us by your power" (Psalm 60:5 NLT). David was a powerful warrior and a highly successful king, but he knew where his strength came from – God. One of David's greatest fears was that God might ever reject him and remove His favor from him. He even asks God, "Have you rejected us, O God? Will you no longer march with our armies?" (Psalm 60:11 NLT). David knew the ramifications if that were ever to happen and it made him shudder. He knew that their existence was based solely on the favor and power of God, not him. Without God, David was nothing, and he knew it. Without God, the nation of Israel was nothing, and David understood that sobering fact as well. So he calls out to God, "Oh, please help us against our enemies, for all human help is useless" (Psalm 60:11 NLT). David knew what we need to know. Without God's help, we are helpless and hopeless. We are His people. He is our King. It is He who protects us, provides for us, gives us victory, keeps us safe, and meets all our needs. It is to Him we should turn in both the good times and the bad times. All human help is useless. Placing our hope in anyone or anything other than God will always prove dangerous and highly disappointing. We may win the battle, but we will end up losing the war. But David knew that "with God's help we will do mighty things, for he will trample down our foes" (Psalm 60:12 NLT). Even this powerful king knew that he was nothing without the help of his all-powerful God.

Father, how ludicrous it is to think that I can somehow save myself. How silly for me to imagine that I can somehow come up with a plan to save myself from all the enemies I face every day. Without You I am nothing. I have no strength without You. I have no wisdom apart from You. I have no future unless You provide it. I have no hope other than You. But with Your help I will do mighty things! Amen

PSALM 60 – DAY 2

We Will Do Mighty Things.
Based on Psalm 60

O God, our sin stinks so bad You can hardly stand to be around us,
So You have ended up scattering us in Your anger.
I ask that You would restore us.
Even the earth seems to shake and tremble before You,
You split it open, and only You can restore it.
You have allowed your people to go through difficult times,
It has left us unstable and staggering like we're drunk on wine.
But for those who fear You, You have given them a banner to display,
That contains the truths of Your promises.
You will deliver those You love.
I beg You to save us by the power of Your hand.
You have spoken from Your throne,
"I will triumph! I will plunder Shechem!
I will portion out the Valley of Succoth as I see fit!
Gilead and Manasseh belong to Me!
Ephraim is like my helmet and Judah my scepter.
Moab will be like a pot where I do my dirty laundry,
Edom will feel the heel of my boot,
And I will triumph over Philistia."
But I can't help but ask You, O God,
Who will make it possible for us to enter a fortified city?
Who will lead us into Edom?
It has to be You, but it appears that You have rejected us,
And that You no longer go out with our armies.
I beg You to give us help against our enemies,
Because any help we receive from man is useless.
But You make us like a mighty army,
You make it possible for us to experience victory over our enemies.

PSALM 60 – DAY 3

Write Psalm 60 in your own words or write a psalm of your own. Be honest and open. Don't be afraid to tell God how you feel, but also include praise for who He is and all that He has done and is going to do in your life.

PSALM 61 – DAY 1

Overwhelmed, But Never Overlooked.

From the ends of the earth, I cry to you for help when my heart is overwhelmed. Lead me to the towering rock of safety. – Psalm 61:2 NLT

David is under tremendous pressure. He is feeling completely overwhelmed by his circumstances. The Hebrew word he uses to describe the condition of his heart means, "to be wrapped in darkness, to languish, to faint."[13] He is in a dark moment of the soul, a time when all looked hopeless and he was feeling helpless. But what does he do at that moment? Does he give up? No, he looks up. He calls out. He cries out to God. "O God, listen to my cry! Hear my prayer!" (Psalm 60:1 NLT). He takes the darkness of his situation to the one source that can shed some light on his condition. He longs for safety and security – a place where his enemies can't reach him and he can enjoy peace from all the turmoil. David knew that his only hope was to be found in God. Keep in mind, this man was a highly successful warrior, a powerful king, and a man who was not afraid to strap on the sword and fight his way out of difficult circumstances. But in this case, he knew that God was his only hope. As he had done so many times before in other psalms, David appeals to God's unfailing love and faithfulness. He asks God to extend his life and prolong his kingdom, so that he can continue to praise and serve Him. David doesn't just want long life in order to enjoy all the things that life has to offer. He wants to be able to continue his life of service to God, keeping his vows and praising Him for all that He has done.

But the truth is, we often beg God to save us in order that we might continue a life that is focused on *us*, not Him. We long for God to rescue us from our difficult circumstances, not so that we can serve Him more, but just so that we might enjoy life on our own terms. Whatever the circumstances were in David's life, he more than likely was not able to

---

[13] "H5848 - `ataph – Strong's Hebrew Lexicon (KJV)." Blue Letter Bible. Web. 9 Aug, 2016. <https://www.blueletterbible.org

worship in the Tabernacle. He was not able to offer sacrifices to God. He was isolated from the presence of God's glory that dwelt in the inner recesses of the Tabernacle. He longed to return home and worship God. He wanted to see his life preserved, so that He might praise God more. What is your motivation for calling on God? Why do you want Him to save you? Is it in order that You might see His power on display and so that you might worship Him? Or is it simply so that you might get back to enjoying life and escaping the inconvenient circumstances in which you find yourself? David's focus was on God. Yes, he wanted God to rescue and preserve him, but only so that he might spend his life serving and praising God.

Father, how often I beg You to save me when my only motivation is to get back to life as usual. My focus is not on You, but me. I simply want to enjoy life, not Your presence. Give me a new perspective. Give me a heart like David's that desires long life so that I might have more time to serve and praise You. Amen

PSALM 61 – DAY 2

I Cry To You.
Based on Psalm 61

O God, I ask you to not only hear my cry, but to respond.
Please pay attention to what I am praying.
When I find myself in extreme circumstances, I will call out to You,
When my heart is overcome by the darkness, and I begin to despair,
Lead me back to the safety of Your greatness,
Where I will find refuge and protection,
Above all my circumstances, exalted above my situations.
For You have always proven to be a shelter for me,
A tower of strength and safety from the enemy.
I will seek refuge in Your presence forever,
I will hide under the protection of Your wings.
You have heard what I have promised,
And You have promised to give me an inheritance
Along with all those who love You and fear You.
Let the king live a long time and impact many generations.
He will live obediently in Your presence,
All I ask is that You watch over Him with Your mercy and truth.
As a result, I will sing praises forever regarding Your reputation,
And I will do what I have promised every day I am alive.

PSALM 61 – DAY 3

Write Psalm 61 in your own words or write a psalm of your own. Be honest and open. Don't be afraid to tell God how you feel, but also include praise for who He is and all that He has done and is going to do in your life.

PSALM 62 – DAY 1

Patiently, Expectantly Waiting.

Let all that I am wait quietly before God, for my hope is in him. He alone is my rock and my salvation, my fortress where I will not be shaken. – Psalm 62:5-6 NLT

For most of us, waiting on God is viewed as some kind of punishment or penance we must pay for our bad behavior. We view it as if God is somehow holding out on us, making us sweat and suffer as He delays giving us what we want in order to teach a lesson. But that perspective is based on a faulty view of God. He is not some petty deity using His power maliciously or malevolently in order to get out of us what He wants from us. He is a loving, patient, merciful God whose actions are always driven by His care and concern for us. For if God was withholding from us what we needed, just in order to punish us or teach us a lesson, what kind of God would He be? Jesus pointed this out when He said, "You parents – if your children ask for a loaf of bread, do you give them a stone instead? Or if they ask for a fish, do you give them a snake? Of course not! So if you sinful people know how to give good gifts to your children, how much more will your heavenly Father give good gifts to those who ask him" (Matthew 7:9-11 NLT). Does that mean we always get what we ask for or that it comes exactly when we expect it? Of course not. God is still God. He is all-knowing and aware of things that are beyond our ability to comprehend. He has a "big picture view" of things that we don't have. He is not bound by space and time, but knows the future as well as He knows the past or present. He is not even limited by our decisions or bad choices. He is in control at all times. At no point is God ever up in heaven wringing His hands in disbelief because He was somehow caught off guard by the events or circumstances surrounding our lives.

So David says, "I wait quietly before God, for my victory comes from Him" (Psalm 62:1 NLT). I love how *The Message* paraphrases that verse: "God, the one and only – I'll wait as long as he says. Everything I need comes from him, so why not?" I'll wait as long as he says. Why? Because He knows best and He has my best in mind. He is my hope and salvation.

He is my help and source of healing. He has a plan for my life that is perfect and complete. So David reminds us, "O my people, trust in him at all times. Pour out your heart to him, for God is our refuge" (Psalm 62:8 NLT). Trust in him at all times. Not just in the good times, but at all times. Even when things seem to be going poorly. Even when it appears as if He is nowhere to be found. Even when everything is going against you and everyone seems to be deserting you. Wait quietly and trust Him. It is in those moments of waiting and trusting that we truly come to know who He really is. It is in quietly waiting that He reminds us of His love and then rewards us with His perfect answer at the perfect time. What we need is NOT the answer we're hoping for, but the God who provides the answer. We need to know Him better. We need to trust Him more. We need to patiently wait and eagerly anticipate an answer because we know the character of our God. His love never fails.

Father, thank You for the moments of waiting that come into my life on a regular basis. Thank You for teaching me to rely on You and not the world around me. May I continue to learn to wait patiently and expectantly on You because I believe You have my best in mind, in spite of what I see happening around me. Amen

PSALM 62 – DAY 2

A Quiet, Patient Hope.
Based on Psalm 62

I am learning to wait quietly and confidently in the Lord,
Because He is my only source of true salvation.
I don't find strength, deliverance, or refuge anywhere else.
He alone keeps me from being shaken by this world.
And I have a message for my enemies:
How long are you going to keep attacking me?
You're all out to break me, but be careful,
To God, your defenses are like an unstable wall or a fence that is about to fall down.
You plot among yourselves about how to bring me down.
You're nothing but liars, always talking trash about me,
Except when you're in my company, then you act like my friends.
But I am learning to wait quietly and confidently in the Lord,
Because my hope comes from Him.
I don't find strength, deliverance, or refuge anywhere else.
He alone keeps me from being shaken by this world.
God provides me with salvation, dignity, a source of strength, and a refuge.
Those who claim to believe in Him should trust Him all the time.
Pour out your heart to Him, because He really is a shelter in the storm.
All men, regardless of their status, are worthless, like a mist.
They deceive and lie, and their combined worth is that of air.
Don't put your confidence in getting ahead through immoral means.
Even if you're fortunate enough to gain wealth, don't rely on it.
I've heard it said that true strength belongs to God alone, and so does mercy.
I've also heard it said that God pays back men according to their deeds.
He is merciful, but He is also just.

PSALM 62 – DAY 3

Write Psalm 62 in your own words or write a psalm of your own. Be honest and open. Don't be afraid to tell God how you feel, but also include praise for who He is and all that He has done and is going to do in your life.

PSALMS 63-64 – DAY 1

Obsessed With God.

I lie awake at night thinking of you, meditating on you through the night. – Psalm 63:6 NLT

I wish I could say that the statement found in the verse above was true of me. But rarely do I find myself lying in bed meditating or thinking about God. Oh, I may find myself thinking about all the things I need God to do for me, but that is not the same thing. I often find myself talking to Him, making requests and asking questions about why things are the way they are and what He is going to do about it all. But David seems to be saying something completely different. Like a child lying awake in bed on Christmas Eve, anticipating the joys of the morning to come, David finds himself immersed in the greatness and goodness of God Himself. He says, "My soul thirsts for you, my whole body longs for you in this parched and weary land where there is no water" (Psalm 63:1 NLT). David is in the midst of trying times, living in a wilderness environment, both literally and figuratively. He is miles from the tabernacle and far from the presence of his own people. Even though he was surrounded by those who have aligned themselves with his cause, David still struggled with feeling alone and isolated. So he found himself staying up at night thinking about God – His power, glory, unfailing love, protection, mercy, and ultimate salvation. Even in the midst of difficulty, David could sing about the goodness of God. He focused his attention on God instead of his circumstances. He thought about the character of God instead of worrying about the cares of the day.

David's life was anything but easy, as Psalm 64 clearly illustrates. He still had enemies. He still had difficulties. He still had plenty of reasons to worry, doubt, fear, and despair. But rather than let his attention focus on his problems, He focused on His God. Reflecting on the nature and character of God is the surest way to get our minds off of the worries of this world. Our suffering should drive us to the One who has the capacity to relieve it. Difficulty should motivate us to turn to the One who can do something about it. Trials should encourage us to turn to the One who can perfect us through them. Rather than lie awake at night worrying, wouldn't it make more sense to spend our time worshiping?

Father, thank You for this timely reminder. Help me to cultivate a habit of thinking about You instead of my problems. Let me learn to focus my attention on Your goodness and greatness rather than the difficulties in my life. Amen

PSALMS 63-64– DAY 2

The Thirst Quencher.
Based on Psalm 63

O God, You are my God; my personal God;
I will seek You from the moment I wake up and all day long.
I have unquenchable thirst for You spiritually,
And living in this world that's like a waterless desert and can leave a man faint,
Even my body longs for the physical refreshment You alone can bring.
I am fully aware of Your holiness, Your set-apartness,
Because I have observed Your power and glory first-hand.
I have discovered that Your mercy and goodness makes living worthwhile,
Which is why praise for You comes so easily from my lips.
So I will bend my knee in submission to You as long as I live,
And I will lift up my hands to You in prayer because of Your reputation.
You spiritually satisfy me like a good meal does the body,
And joyful praise is my response.
When I lie in bed at night, my thoughts go to You,
I fill my sleepless nights by thinking about You.
Because You have been my help in the past.
I know I will find myself safely rejoicing in Your protection again.
I hold on to You for dear life,
And You keep me safe in Your powerful grip.
But as far as those who wish to harm me,
You will take care of them, giving them exactly what they deserve.
They will suffer death and defeat, their bodies consumed by wild animals.
But as the king of Your people, I will rejoice in You.
Everyone who is true to their word and follows You will have reason to glory,
But all those who speak falsely will one day be stopped.

Put the Fear of God In Them.
Based on Psalm 64

O God, please listen to what I am saying.
I know it sounds like complaining,
But I need You to keep me from fearing my enemies.
Hide me so that their plots against me fail,
Don't let this unruly mob of hooligans get to me.
They use their tongues like a well-sharpened sword,
Like a bow in an arrow, their bitter words pierce deeply.
They aim them at those who seek to live with integrity,
Attacking suddenly and with impunity.
They seem to find strength in doing what is wrong,
They brag about the traps they secretly set,
Saying, "Who will ever see them?"
They're always seeking new ways to do what is wrong,
And their search is usually successful.
The depth of their thoughts and the hearts behind them are a mystery.
But what they don't know is that God has them in His sights.
They will find themselves wounded, stabbed like an arrow by God Himself.
Their own words will be turned against them,
Others will shudder when they see what happens to them.
All men will end up fearing God when they see what He has done.
They will have to think long and hard about His actions.
Those who are righteous in God's eyes will rejoice in Him,
They'll learn to put their hope and trust in Him.
Those whose hearts are right with God will have reason to boast in Him.

PSALM 63-64 – DAY 3

Write Psalm 63 in your own words or write a psalm of your own. Be honest and open. Don't be afraid to tell God how you feel, but also include praise for who He is and all that He has done and is going to do in your life.

PSALM 63-64 – DAY 3

Write Psalm 64 in your own words or write a psalm of your own. Be honest and open. Don't be afraid to tell God how you feel, but also include praise for who He is and all that He has done and is going to do in your life.

PSALM 65 – DAY 1

As If Forgiveness Was Not Enough.

Though we are overwhelmed by our sins, you forgive them all. – Psalm 65:3 NLT

Sinfulness is the one characteristic we all share as human beings. And forgiveness from our sins is the one thing we all must receive from God if we are to live in harmony with Him. But in order for us to have a right relationship with God, our sin problem had to be taken care of first. The penalty for our sin – death – had to be paid in full. And God took care of it by sending His Son to die in our place on the cross. Because of Jesus' substitutionary death on the cross for us, we had our sin payment paid in full. And not only the sins of the past, but the sins yet to be committed. That is why we can bring any sin to Him and receive forgiveness. Like David, we can feel overwhelmed by our sin and still receive forgiveness from God. All we need to do is confess them – admit that what we have done was a sin against Him. And the amazing thing is that God forgives us each and every time.

But as amazing as forgiveness of sin is, we can sometimes forget that God's mercy shows up in our lives in so many other ways that we take for granted. David reminds us that God not only forgives our sins, He answers our prayers. "You faithfully answer our prayers with awesome deeds" (Psalm 65:5 NLT). We pray. God answers. And He answers according to His power. God does great and mighty things when we pray and place ourselves at His mercy. But that's not all. God has surrounded us with signs of His power. The mountains and the oceans, the rising and setting sun, the rain and the rivers. The way He can turn a dry valley into a lush pasture, providing food for a flock of grazing sheep. His faithfulness in causing crops to grow and the earth to provide much-needed resources for life to continue on this planet. When David saw all that God did on a daily basis for mankind, he said, "you inspire shouts of joy!" (Psalm 65:8 NLT). You would think forgiveness of sin and the gift of salvation would be enough. But God continues to pour out His blessings on men in so many ways. All we enjoy on this earth is a gift *from* Him. Everything that exists was created *by* Him. The wonders of this world remind us constantly *of* Him. He is a great, good, faithful and forgiving God who inspires shouts of joy!

Father, while I am eternally grateful for Your forgiveness of my sins, I don't ever want to take for granted all the other wonders You work in and around my life each and every day. You are a merciful, loving God who has given mankind so much. You provided us with life and then You surrounded us with the awe of Your creation. Even with the effects of the fall, this world is still a pretty amazing place in which to live. We get to see Your power and experience Your provision each and every day. So not only do I get to enjoy Your forgiveness, I get to live in the midst of Your creation. Amen

PSALM 65 – DAY 2

The Bountiful Blessings of God.
Based on Psalm 65

My praise waits silently, expectantly on You, O God,
And I will fulfill all my vows to You.
You are the one who hears and answers prayers,
So all men must come to You eventually.
Your words regarding my sins are too much for me,
But You make atonement for all my transgressions against You!
Happy is the man You choose to offer a relationship with You,
Who You allow to stand in Your presence.
The goodness that is found where You are will satisfy each and every one of us,
Even in the house of God.
You prove You are our salvation every day by awe-inspiring acts of justice.
You are the hope of all mankind, whether they are on the land or the sea.
The mountains are an exhibition of Your great power,
You can control and even calm the raging waters of the oceans,
And you can handle the raging multitudes just as easily.
Even men living in the remotest parts of the world are awed by Your signs,
As they rejoice in the beauty of Your sunrises and sunsets.
You care for the earth, providing it with rain,
Enriching it with the rivers You have created.
You provide men with grain and corn, which You have prepared for them.
You even water the fields that men have prepared,
Softening the soil and causing the crops to grow.
You crown the year with abundance,
And leave blessing everywhere You go.
From meadows in the middle of nowhere to remote mountaintops,
Your blessings rain down.
The pastures are clothed with flocks,
The valleys are covered over with corn,
Visually shouting Your praises and reflecting the joy of Your goodness.

PSALM 65 – DAY 3

Write Psalm 65 in your own words or write a psalm of your own. Be honest and open. Don't be afraid to tell God how you feel, but also include praise for who He is and all that He has done and is going to do in your life.

PSALM 66 – DAY 1

Keeping Your Testimony Current.

Come and listen, all you who fear God, and I will tell you what he did for me. – Psalm 66:16 NLT

What has God done for you lately? That should be an easy question for any Christ-follower to answer. Because the reality is, God is acting on our behalf each and every day in countless ways. But the sad truth is that we oftentimes fail to see His hand in our lives. Other times we simply fail to ask for God's assistance with the affairs of life. We go it alone. We muddle on through life, attempting to take on all our problems by ourselves, ignoring the ready availability of His power, grace and mercy. For many of us, our testimony is a dusty, faded photograph that captures some event that happened years ago in our lives. It was momentous, life-changing and an unforgettable experience, but it is still a distant memory. Much time has passed since our conversion experience. We have lived more years than we would like to remember, experienced the ups and downs of life, and, hopefully, grown in our knowledge and understanding of God. But if someone walked up and asked us what God had done for us lately, what would we have to say? How would we answer?

For David, it would have been a simple question and he would have had a ready response. He said, "Come and listen, all you who fear God, and I will tell you what he did for me" (Psalm 66:16 NLT). David had a story to tell, a recollection to recount, of what God had done in his life. And as we have worked our way through the psalms of David, we have seen plenty of proof that David had ample stories to share of God's goodness, grace, mercy, power and provision. God was actively involved in David's life. His response to the question, "What has God done for you lately?," would probably have been, "How much time do you have?" In this psalm David talks of the glory of God's name. He expresses how glorious God is. He exclaims, "How awesome are your deeds!" (Psalm 66:3 NLT). He invites others to "Come and see what our God has done, what awesome miracles he performs for people!" (Psalm 66:5 NLT). David can recount what God has done in the past for His people. But David can also share what God has done more recently in his own life. And that is the story most people want and need to hear. A lost and dying world is looking for a living, active God who is engaged on a daily basis with those who worship Him. Don't misunderstand me, our salvation story is significant. But God didn't stop saving us at conversion. He is still redeeming, rescuing, refining and restoring us each and every day of our lives. He is disciplining us, teaching us, constantly forgiving us, leading and directing us, healing and helping us, and daily molding us into the likeness of His Son. Like David, we should be able to say, "Come and listen, all you who fear God, and I will tell you what he did for me." We are proof of God's presence. Our daily lives should be evidence of His love, grace, mercy, power, forgiveness and, ultimately, of His existence. So what has God done for you lately? Great! Now go tell someone.

Father, You have given me ample stories to tell of Your presence in my life. Forgive me for not telling others. You have proven Yourself faithful to me time and time again, but I don't always pass that news along to those around me. Place in me a growing desire to sing Your praises to all those willing to listen. Create in me a desire to talk You up on a consistent basis. May I become increasingly more a satisfied customer — the best advertising of Your power, presence and provision. Amen

PSALM 66 – DAY 2

Prayer = Praise.
Based on Psalm 66

Shout joyfully in praise to God, everybody and everything on earth!
Sing songs about the glory of His reputation,
And when you do it, make your praise of Him glorious and abundant.
Tell Him how awe-inspiring His deeds are,
And that His great power causes His enemies to cringe before Him.
Sing, "Everyone and everything on earth will bow down before You,
And one day they will all sing Your praises."
Come and consider all that God does,
What He does among men is both awe-inspiring and fear-producing.
He turned an uncrossable sea into dry land so the Israelites could pass through.
The result was a lot of rejoicing!
His power allows Him to rule for all time – uninterrupted,
He constantly keeps watch over the nations of the earth,
So those who rebel against Him have no business getting full of themselves.
As His people, it is our job to bless Him and make His praises known.
He is the one who gives us life and preserves us,
He keeps us from falling.
O God, You have tried us and proved us,
You have refined us like silver is refined.
You were with us when we ended up in the trap.
It was Your idea to use this pressure in our lives.
You allowed others to lord it over us,
We passed through fire and water,
But in the end, You brought us into a better place.
So I will worship You and fulfill all my commitments to You.
Every promise I made to You when I was in trouble, I will keep.
I will offer up to You the sacrifices You require, whatever the cost.
If You fear God and love Him, come and listen to all I have to say about Him,
Come listen to what He has done in my life.
I cried out to Him for help, and ended up praising Him for what He did.
But unconfessed sin in my life would have prevented that from happening.

But God not only heard me, He answered me.
So I bless and praise God who did not reject my prayer
Or withhold His mercy from me.

PSALM 66 – DAY 3

Write Psalm 66 in your own words or write a psalm of your own. Be honest and open. Don't be afraid to tell God how you feel, but also include praise for who He is and all that He has done and is going to do in your life.

PSALM 67 – DAY 1

Making God Known.

May your ways be known throughout the earth, your saving power among people everywhere. – Psalm 67:2 NLT

This ought to be the daily prayer of every child of God. There should be a deep desire in each and every one of us that God would reveal Himself, make Himself known, to every person that walks the face of the earth. The Scriptures clearly teach that God is revealed through His creation. "For ever since the world was created, people have seen the earth and sky. Through everything God made, they can clearly see his invisible qualities – his eternal power and divine nature. So they have no excuse for not knowing God" (Revelation 1:20 NLT). God's power and character are revealed in His creation. But those same qualities should be revealed in us as human beings – the pinnacle of His creation. After all, we are made in His image. And those of us who have been redeemed by the death of His Son and given the indwelling presence of His Spirit should be daily illustrations of His power and character. Others should be able to see Him at work in us and around us.

David prays, "May your ways be known throughout the earth, your saving power among people everywhere." Interestingly, David uses the word, "ways," which in the Hebrew can refer to a journey, path, or course of life. It can also refer to the habits or manner in which one performs his or her duties. It seems that David is referring to the "way" in which God relates to His people – through His saving power. That is what David wants the world to see. The NET Bible notes that David's use of that specific word "refers here to God's characteristic behavior, more specifically, to the way he typically saves his people."[14] David wants the world to be able to see God's mercy, grace, forgiveness, kindness and saving power as He rescues

---

[14] *Holy Bible,* New Living Translation, copyright © 1996, 2004, 2015 by Tyndale House Foundation. Used by permission of Tyndale House Publishers Inc., Carol Stream, Illinois 60188

His people. Of course, behind this request is a desire to be saved by God. David wants to see God work in his own life and in the lives of the people of God. He realizes that when the nations see the kind of God the people of Israel serve, they will end up praising Him, too. They will be able to see that He rules with justice, that He is powerful, and that He uses that power to care for those who worship Him.

We should desire for God to make Himself known through us. But think about that. That means we should be ready and willing to find ourselves in situations in which we *have to* rely on God for salvation. We have to be willing to suffer circumstances in which God can reveal His saving power in our lives. Had the Israelites not found themselves at the Red Sea with the army of Egypt bearing down on them, they would never have witnessed the saving power of God. Their difficulty proved to be an opportunity to witness the "ways" of God. Had David not found himself on the run with a bounty on his head, fleeing from King Saul, he would never have known the "ways" of God. The truth is, the unwanted ways in which our lives sometimes go are exactly where God wants us so that He can reveal His "ways" through us and to us. God is making Himself known throughout the world, and He is doing it through us, His people. We are to be revealers of His power, mercy, grace, and saving power.

Father, make Yourself known through me today. Use the circumstances of my life to reveal Your ways to the world around me. May Your saving power be evident to everyone who sees me today, including me. Amen

PSALM 67 – DAY 2

Making His Ways Known.
Based on Psalm 67

God, I ask You to show mercy on us and bless us,
To look down on us and show us Your favor.
That the world might see Your true character as You work through us,
Your salvation revealed to a watching world.
Cause the nations of the world to confess Your greatness, O God,
Give them plenty of reasons to praise You.
Cause the people of the world to rejoice,
Shouting joyfully as they see You work among them.
For You judge righteously, leading and guiding all those who live on the earth.
Give Your people cause to praise You, O God,
Give them plenty of reasons to praise You!
Just as the earth faithfully produces crops for us,
So our God will bless us.
He will bless us,
And everyone living on the earth will learn to honor, fear, and respect Him.

PSALM 67 – DAY 3

Write Psalm 67 in your own words or write a psalm of your own. Be honest and open. Don't be afraid to tell God how you feel, but also include praise for who He is and all that He has done and is going to do in your life.

PSALM 68 – DAY 1

You're In Good Hands.

Praise the Lord; praise God our savior! For each day he carries us in his arms. – Psalm 68:19 NLT

What has become an easily recognizable tagline for an insurance company could more readily be said of God. You're in good hands with … God. David reminds us that our God carries us each and every day. He paints the picture of a shepherd carrying a sheep in his arms, protecting it, providing for it, and ensuring that it gets where it needs to go. Our great God carries us. What a picture of intimacy and love, but what a reminder of God's matchless power. In this psalm, David speaks of God's great power, the same power that freed the Israelites from Egypt, led them to the Promised Land, and conquered their enemies living there. This great, majestic, powerful God is also "Father to the fatherless, defender of widows," who "places the lonely in families; he sets the prisoner free and gives them joy" (Psalm 68:5-6 NLT). He is not a distant deity who reigns from some unseen place and dispenses justice and judgment like some invisible judge. He is with us and for us. From the moment He chose Abram to be the father of the Hebrew nation, God has lived in and among men. Throughout the wilderness wandering years, God traveled with the people of Israel, leading the way, taking the form of a pillar of smoke by day and a pillar of fire by night. They always knew He was with them. When He instructed Moses to build the tabernacle in the wilderness, He came to dwell within the Holy of Holies, a constant reminder of His presence and power. Later, God's presence would fill the Holy of Holies of the new temple constructed by King Solomon. "Now the Lord will live among us there" (Psalm 68:18 NLT). God chose to dwell among men. He made His presence known and displayed His power among them. "God is awesome in his sanctuary. The God of Israel gives power and strength to his people" (Psalm 68:35 NLT).

We are in good hands with God. He is powerful, but also gentle. He is majestic, but also intimate. He delivers judgment with a firm hand, but He also metes out justice with tender mercy. He has the power to destroy our enemies, and the compassion to forgive us of our sins. He can rain down judgment, but also deliver rain to restore a dry land. Our God is great, but this great God cares for us. That should blow us away. It should cause us to respond in praise, prayer, gratitude, joy, hope and worship. "Praise the Lord; praise God our savior! For each day he carries us in his arms" (Psalms 68:19 NLT).

Father, thank You for this much-needed reminder. I am in Your arms, therefore I am safe. You are taking me where I need to go. You are protecting me at all times. You are healing me, holding me and helping me. I have nothing to fear, but much for which to be grateful. Amen

PSALM 68 – DAY 2

Our Great God.
Based on Psalm 68

Show up! O God! Make an appearance and cause Your enemies to run.
Make all those who hate You run from Your presence.
Cause them to disappear like smoke in the wind,
Let them melt away like wax in the presence of a flame.
May all those who are hostile to You vanish from before You.
But give the righteous plenty of reasons to rejoice in Your presence.
Let them be glad that they can even come into Your presence.
Let them sing praises for Your great reputation,
Praising you, the transcendent God, in Your very presence.
You lovingly father the fatherless. righteously provide justice for widows,
You rule and reign in holiness.
You put those who are alone in families,
You free those who are imprisoned,
But You cast those who rebel against You into the wilderness.
O God, You've always gone before Your people,
Like the time You led them in their own wilderness wanderings.
It was a time of earth-shaking and manna-making,
Even Mount Sinai shook before Your presence, O God of Israel.
You caused refreshing rain to fall in times of dryness,
Confirming this land as the inheritance of Your people.
And there they've lived, as You have shown Your goodness in the midst of their poverty.
You spoke and there was a huge host to spread the word abroad.
Kings and their armies ran away from You, leaving the spoil for our women to pick up.
Even the poorest of the poor found treasures of silver and gold.
You scattered the kings like snow before the wind on Mount Zalmon.
Mount Sinai, where You dwell is as high as the Mountain of Bashan,
Other mountains look with envy, because God has chosen to make His permanent
*   dwelling in His holy hill.*
He has tens of thousands of chariots and just as many angels,
All at His disposal on Mount Sinai. His holy place.
He dwells at the pinnacle, where He has led His captives,
Where men give Him gifts, even from the rebellious.

You live among men in Your holy place.
You deserve our praise because You carry our burdens each and every day,
You are our salvation!
You are our God, the God who saves, who even delivers from death.
But You will destroy Your enemies, all those who stubbornly resist You.
You will seek and destroy them all, wherever they may be.
Like a victorious king, You will wade through their blood, and your dogs will consume
    their remains.
They have all seen what You do, O God, what You do from Your holy sanctuary.
They have seen the processions complete with singers, musicians and women with
    tamborines.
They have witnesses the huge congregations of Your people worshiping You.
From the little tribe of Benjamin, home of Your chosen ruler,
To the princes of Judah, Zebulun and Napthtali.
You are the God who has given them all their strength,
Now we ask that You reveal Your power.
Kings will bring tributes to You at Your temple in Jerusalem.
Humble and humiliate these wild animals, these bulls with their calves,
Let them bring their silver and gold as penalty for their love affair with war.
Princes from as far away as Egypt and Ethiopia will bring their tributes to You.
They will all end up singing Your praises.
They will praise Him who rides on high, above the heavens,
Where He thunders loudly and powerfully.
Give God credit for His power, His sovereignty over Israel,
Even the power He displays in the skies.
You are an awesome God, who displays Your strength and power to Your people,
Which is why we praise and bless You.

PSALM 68 – DAY 3

Write Psalm 68 in your own words or write a psalm of your own. Be honest and open. Don't be afraid to tell God how you feel, but also include praise for who He is and all that He has done and is going to do in your life.

PSALM 69 – DAY 1

Living Lessons.

The humble will see their God at work and be glad. Let all who seek God's help be encouraged. – Psalm 69:32 NLT

Do you ever wonder why difficulty comes into your life? As a Christian, do you ever question why God would allow you to suffer at all? Pain, persecution and trials of all kinds are difficult for us to handle, even as Christ-followers. As human beings we seem innately wired to run from trouble, or to confront it head on. In either case, our intent is to escape it or remove it from our lives. Yet this reality of pain and suffering is one of the things we human beings all have in common. Yes, it comes in varying degrees of difficulty and some seem to suffer more than others. But no one gets to go through life completely untouched by sorrow, hurt, difficulty, trials, and the feelings of despair they bring.

Even as God's anointed king of Israel, David was not immune to difficulty. In fact, long before his kingdom began, he found himself in dire straights, running for his life and spending his days living in the wilderness instead of a palace. Psalm 69 reflects the words of a man who is in deep trouble. He is up to his neck in difficulty. We don't know the circumstances surrounding his situation, but it is clear that David is having a hard time. He says, "I am in deep water," "I sink into the mire," I am exhausted," "I weep and fast," and "I am in despair." Things are not going well for David, and so he is calling out to His God for help. He asks God to save him, rescue him, to show him favor, to answer his prayer and show him favor. He appeals to God's unfailing love and mercy. David knows that God is his only hope. He fully understands that God alone has the power to rescue him from all that is happening to him. While David doesn't enjoy what is going on, he sees it as an opportunity to watch God work. He knows that this is a chance to witness the power of God displayed in and around his life. His pain and suffering provide a platform on which God can display His power. And when God does rescue, David will have plenty of reasons to praise and thank God. Not only that, all those who love and honor God will also have ample reason to be encouraged and emboldened to trust God too. David knew that his difficulties were simply temporal occasions for God to display His eternal power. Our trials are no trouble for God. He is not worried, dismayed, in panic, or fearful about the outcome. He simply wants to reveal His strength through our weakness. He wants to display His power through our impotence. God loves to save. He longs to rescue. And when His children praise and thank Him when He does, He is glorified and honored. When God rescues us, others are encouraged. When God intervenes on our behalf and we sing His praises to those around us, they are prompted to trust in God the next time they go through trials and difficulties. Our troubles become opportunities to witness of God's saving power. They provide us with real-life examples of God's presence and provision. They remind us of God's love and mercy. And when we thank Him for His salvation from trouble, and tell others what He has done for us, He is glorified. And all who seek God's help get encouraged.

Father, You long to intervene in our lives and You long to show Your power. You have chosen to do so through our weaknesses. You have determined to display Your glory through those events in our lives that reveal our own weaknesses. May we see those times as opportunities to see You work. And when You do, may we give You the glory and praise You deserve. So that others will be encouraged to trust You more. Amen

PSALMS 69 – DAY 2

It's Never So Bad That God Can't Do Good.
Based on Psalm 69

Save me, O God,
For the waters of difficulty are flooding my soul.
It's like I am sinking into a bottomless mud pit.
I find myself in deep waters that flow over my head.
I have been calling for help so long my throat hurts and I am exhausted,
Even my eyes grow weary looking for your salvation to come.
It seems like there are more people who hate me without cause
Than there are hairs on my head.
These enemies who would destroy me, even though I don't deserve it,
They make me pay back a debt I never owed.
O God, You know every foolish thing I've ever done,
And none of my sins are hidden from You.
Don't let all those who hope in and wait on You be disappointed because of me,
Don't let those who seek You be ashamed because of me.
For it's because of You that I suffer all this contempt,
It is for Your sake that I am disgraced.
I am like a stranger to those who I used to call friends,
And a foreigner to my own family.
My unbridled love for Your house has ended up devouring me,
And all the scorn they have for You is now directed at me.
Even when I cry and fast, all I get is insults.
I mourn my circumstances, and they ridicule me.
The well-respected gossip about me,
While the drunks make up songs about me.
But as for me, I pray to You and ask that Your answer come at a favorable time.
Show me mercy, answer me by showing me Your salvation.
Rescue me out of the mud and don't let me sink any further.
Deliver me out of the deep water, from those who hate me without cause.
Don't let the waters of adversity overcome me,
Don't let me be swallowed up or sink down.
Hear me, O God, because of Your love,

Turn to me and rescue me out of Your great compassion.
Don't turn Your face away from Your servant,
I am in trouble; hear me and answer quickly.
Draw near to my soul and deliver it,
Redeem it, and rescue me from my enemies.
You understand full well all that I am going through,
The insults, reproach, shame and dishonor.
You're very familiar with all my enemies, because they are Yours, too.
I am brokenhearted because of the constant scorn,
My soul is sick, and I long for someone to show me pity.
I long for compassion, but there in none coming.
Instead, they feed me a steady diet of poison,
They give me vinegar to drink.
May what they serve up to me become a trap for them.
And may all they hoped to gain from this turn against them.
Blind their eyes, let them shake with fear.
Pour out Your divine judgment on them;
Let them experience Your just anger.
May their homes become desolate and their tents empty.
For they take joy in harassing the one You have chosen to discipline,
And they gossip about the one You have punished.
Repay them to the same degree they have paid me,
Don't let any of them enjoy Your salvation.
Don't let their names be written in the Book of Life, blot them out.
But I am poor and in pain, so let Your salvation deliver me.
When You do, I will praise You in song and give You thanks,
Which will please You more than any sacrifice I could make.
Others who are weak and powerless will see this and be glad,
And they will be encouraged to seek You as well.
For You hear those in need and do not ignore those imprisoned by pain.
Let heaven and earth praise You, the oceans and everything in them.
For You will save Zion and build the cities of Judah,
So that Your people can live there and call it their permanent possession.
The descendants of Your servants will inherit it,
And all those who love Your name will live there.

PSALM 69 – DAY 3

Write Psalm 69 in your own words or write a psalm of your own. Be honest and open. Don't be afraid to tell God how you feel, but also include praise for who He is and all that He has done and is going to do in your life.

PSALM 70 – DAY 1

The Necessity of Neediness.

But as for me, I am poor and needy; please hurry to my aid, O God. You are my helper and my savior; O Lord, do not delay. – Psalm 70:5 NLT

Who knew David could be a man of few words, but in this Psalm we see him cut to the chase and make his point to God in record time. He doesn't beat around the bush, but instead comes right out and tells God what he wants. "Please God, rescue me!" (Psalm 70:1 NLT). And he asks God to do it quickly. Evidently, David's need is pressing and he feels the pressure to demand immediate action by God. In a psalm of so few words, it is interesting to note what David took the time to say. He expressed his need for God's salvation, his desire for justice for his enemies and, lastly, but probably most importantly, his awareness of his own condition. David says, "I am poor and needy." This short phrase speaks volumes about David's awareness of his condition. There is no hint of pride or self-sufficiency. You see no arrogance in this statement. Instead, it reveals a man who is painfully aware of his status and unashamed to admit it to God. He is the king of Israel, the commander of a great army, living in a beautiful palace surrounded by rich treasures. But inwardly, David knows he is needy, destitute, and unable to meet his real needs. He cannot save himself. He needs God. The key for any of us seeing God work in our lives is coming to the realization that we need Him. And before that can happen, we have to come to the same place David did – where we are ready to acknowledge our need. But that is harder than it sounds for most of us. We tend to want to solve our problems and meet our own needs. We want to rescue ourselves and then pat ourselves on the back for a job well done. It is hard to help someone who refuses to see their need for help. But David had reached the point where he was no longer going to let pride stand in his way. He knew that God was his helper and savior. He knew that there was nothing he could do to solve his problem. He needed God. So he called to Him. And David knew from experience that those who call on God are seldom, if ever, disappointed. "But may all who search for you be filled with joy and gladness in you. May those who love your salvation repeatedly shout, 'God is great!'" (Psalm 70:4 NLT).

Father, it seems the longer I live the more I recognize my true neediness. I guess it is that I am slowly learning the valuable lesson that I cannot save myself. I am not smart enough or powerful enough to rescue myself from the troubles of life. I need You. Thanks for the daily reminders of my own weakness and insufficiency. Help me to keep turning to You for help. Amen

PSALM 70 – DAY 2

I Need You.
Based on Psalm 70

Hurry up, O God, and rescue me!
Hurry up and help me, Lord!
Disappoint and embarrass all those who seek my life.
Turn back and humiliate all those who desire to hurt me.
Let all those who laugh at me be rejected to their own shame.
But let everyone who seeks You rejoice and be glad,
And let all those who love and long for Your salvation be able to say,
"Our God is great!"
As for me, I am poor and in great need,
So hurry God, because You're my only help and salvation.
Do not wait another minute!

PSALM 70 – DAY 3

Write Psalm 70 in your own words or write a psalm of your own. Be honest and open. Don't be afraid to tell God how you feel, but also include praise for who He is and all that He has done and is going to do in your life.

PSALM 86 – DAY 1

Learning How To Really Live.

Teach me your ways, O Lord, that I may live according to your truth! Grant me purity of heart, so that I may honor you. – Psalm 86:11 NLT

Most of us think we know what we want out of life. We have a general idea of the kinds of things it takes to get the most out of our time on this planet. And they usually include some, if not a lot of the following: Possessions, pleasure, prosperity, popularity, and power in some form or fashion. We have been sold a bill of goods that those things are what make life meaningful and bring joy and contentment. But David, as the king of Israel, had all of those things. He was powerful, rich, influential, and popular, but he had learned that all of it was meaningless and incapable of bringing him peace. He knew there was more to life and He knew that God was the source. So he prayed, "O Lord, teach me how you want me to live!" (Psalm 86:11 NET). The Hebrew word David uses conveys the idea of a journey or path. He is asking God to show me which road to take that will lead to the right destination. David has an end in mind, a destination. Possessions, pleasure, prosperity, popularity and power all lead somewhere, to a destination, but is it where God wants us to end up? Will they help us arrive at the place He has in mind for us? These things tend to lead us down the path that ends up in pride, self-sufficiency, enslavement, discontentment, greed, covetousness, jealousy, fear, anxiety, and so much more. So David asks God to point him in the right direction, show him the right path to take that will get him where he needs to be.

David continues his prayer: "...that I may live according to your truth." The Hebrew word translated "live" in this verse is actually a word that means literally "to walk" or figuratively, "to live your life." David knows that living according to God's truth requires walking down the right path. We can't live according to God's will for our lives if we keep doing things our own way or pursuing our own agendas. David understands that it all begins by having God point us in the right direction. We have to know the right path if we are going to walk in the right direction and discover the right way to live. Over in the book of Ephesians, Paul writes to the Gentile believers there reminding them that, "You used to live (*peripateo*) in sin, just like the rest of the world, obeying the devil – the commander of the powers in the unseen world" (Ephesians 2:2 NLT). The Greek word peripateo means "to walk or live your life."[15] He is telling them that there was a time when they lived just like the rest of the world. But now they knew a different way of life, a different path to take. "Therefore I, a prisoner for serving the Lord, beg you to lead a life (*peripateo*) worthy of your calling, for you have been called by God" (Ephesians 4:1 NLT). Now they were to walk differently, according to God's road map for life. This path produces different results. It leads to a different place. It leads to holiness, humility, gentleness, peace, patience, kindness, and unity. It leads to selflessness, not selfishness.

Finally, David asks God, "Grant me purity of heart" (Psalm 86:11 NLT). *The NET Bible* translates this request, "make me wholeheartedly committed to you!"[16] He is asking for an undivided, fully committed heart that will stick to the path that God has shown him. Possessions, pleasure, prosperity, popularity, and power will always be beckoning to us along the way, tempting us to step off of the path pointed out to us by God. We need God to equip us with a single-minded devotion and commitment to remain true to His path and not deviate. His path and His path alone will get us where we need to be. His path will allow us to reach the destination He has in store for us. Any other path will take us places we really don't want to go.

Father, keep me on Your path. Help me take my eyes off those other ways of life that can sometimes look so appealing. Constantly remind me that it is Your way that leads to life. It is Your path that is the only true path to joy, peace, contentment, hope, help, happiness, and eternal life. Amen

---

[15] "G4043 - peripateō – Strong's Greek Lexicon (KJV)." Blue Letter Bible. Web. 9 Aug, 2016. https://www.blueletterbible.org

[16] *NET Bible*, Biblical Studies Press, L.L.C., http://netbible.com

PSALM 86 – DAY 2

What Do I Want From God?
Based on Psalm 86

Turn Your ear to hear my prayer, O Lord;
Please answer me, for I am in sad state and in need of help.
Keep me safe, for I am faithful to You.
O God, save me for I am Your servant and I trust in You.
Show me mercy, O God, for I cry out to you daily.
I am bearing my soul to You, O Lord; restore my joy!
You are good, forgiving, and merciful to all those who call on You.
Hear my prayers, O Lord, and pay attention to my requests for favor.
Whenever I am in trouble, I call on You, because You hear and answer me.
There is no other god like You, and no one does the things You do.
Every people group on the face of the earth that You created will one day worship You,
And will one day honor Your great name, O Lord.
You alone are God and You do great and extraordinary things.
Instruct me in the way You want me to live my life,
And I will continually conduct myself according to Your truth.
I want to reverence Your name with my whole heart.
I will continually praise You with all my heart, O Lord my God;
I will make Your great reputation known every day that I live.
The mercy You have shown me is immeasurable,
You have delivered me from the lowest, darkest place.
The arrogant have stood against me,
And terrifying men who have no place for You in their lives have sought to destroy me;
But You are a gracious God, full of compassion, patient,
And with more than enough mercy and truth to go around.
Turn to me, show me mercy, support me by Your power, and save me.
Show me a sign of Your favor, O Lord,
So that those who hate me might see it and lose heart.
May they realize that You support and comfort me, O Lord.

PSALM 86 – DAY 3

Write Psalm 86 in your own words or write a psalm of your own. Be honest and open. Don't be afraid to tell God how you feel, but also include praise for who He is and all that He has done and is going to do in your life.

PSALM 101 – DAY 1

I Will...

I will be careful to live a blameless life—when will you come to help me? I will lead a life of integrity in my own home. – Psalm 101:2 NLT

What will you do for God? For most of us, we have a long list of things we would like God to do for us. We have prayer requests we would like Him to answer. We have problems we would like Him to solve. We have people in our lives we would like Him to change, conflicts we would like Him to resolve, illnesses we would like Him to heal, mysteries we would like Him to reveal, and cloudy futures we would like Him to clear up. But what are we willing to do for Him? Over and over again in this short psalm, David says, "I will…" David is expressing his willingness to praise God, to pursue a life of integrity, to refuse looking at anything inappropriate, to reject relationships with the wicked, to not tolerate conceit and pride in his life, to search out the faithful as his companions, and to hire those whose lives are above reproach as his employees. What David was telling God was that he was serious about living a life that was set apart for His use. He understood the concept of holiness. David knew that, as God's chosen servant, his life was to be distinctive and different. It was to be characterized by a revolutionary new way of life. David was not doing these things in an attempt to please God or score brownie points with Him, but because they are characteristic of someone who shares God's heart. Back in Psalm 86, David prayed, "Teach me your ways, O Lord, that I may live according to your truth! Great me purity of heart, that I may honor you" (Psalm 86:11 NLT). In Psalm 101, David describes what he has learned about God's way – His path for living life. It is a life characterized by integrity or wholeness. It is "sound" or "healthy" in all areas, not just in parts. There is no compartmentalization or hidden areas where God has no sway or influence. David says, "I will be careful to live a blameless life" He is not promising to live a perfect life, but a whole one. He is saying that he is going to do everything he can to live a life that will bring glory to God in every detail. David goes on to tell God, "I will lead a life of integrity in my own home." That word translated "integrity" shares the same root word as the one

320

translated "blameless" earlier in the verse. Again, it has to do with wholeness and completeness. David is expressing his desire to live a holy, set-apart life in every area of his life – even at home, where no one else can see him.

There is a sense in which we will have to make difficult decisions if we want to live according to God's way. Like David, we will have to "refuse to look at anything vile and vulgar" (Psalm 101:3 NLT). Think about that the next time you turn on the TV or head to the movie theater. We will have to "hate all who deal crookedly" and "have nothing to do with them" (Psalm 101:3 NLT). David is not telling us to hate the lost, but to refuse to enjoy the companionship of those whose lives dishonor God. Do you enjoy the company of those who have no heart for the things of God. Do you actually prefer being with them more than you enjoy the company of believers? David seems to be speaking more about having a love affair with their behavior than with the individuals themselves. Are the lifestyles of the godless more appealing to us than those of the godly? David said, "I will search for faithful people to be my companions" (Psalm 101:6 NLT). He wanted to hang with the holy, not the heathen.

David wanted his life to be different, so he was willing to make changes to the way he lived. He sought new habits and new friends. He chose to give up old ways of doing things. He made a conscious decision to surround himself with good influences. What are you willing to do for God? What steps are you willing to take to ensure that your life is marked by integrity and wholeness?

Father, You want all of my life, not just the parts that people see on Sunday morning. You desire that I would be willing to make changes to the way that I live. You have given me a new heart and the power to live differently, but I still have to choose to do so. And it begins with the daily decisions to live my whole life for You. Amen

PSALM 101 – DAY 2

I Will...
Based on Psalm 101

I will sing about Your mercy and just judgment, O God.
I will praise You in song.
I will be careful to live my whole life in a wise and understanding way.
When will You come to rescue me?
In the meantime, I will live my life with integrity even when I am home alone.
I won't allow anything dishonest or questionable into my life.
I will despise the things done by those who oppose You,
And not let their actions become a part of my life.
I will not tolerate fraud in my heart,
I will not be known for having an evil heart.
I will not have anything to do with those who slander others,
And I will not put up with the haughty and arrogant.
Instead, I will make believers the focus of my attention.
I will spend my time with those whose lives model integrity,
They will minister beside me and to me.
But I won't have anything to do with those who can't be trusted,
Whose words and lives fail to model integrity.
I will make it my mission in life to remove all evil influences from my life.
No one who loves wickedness will not be tolerated in my world.

PSALM 101 – DAY 3

Write Psalm 101 in your own words or write a psalm of your own. Be honest and open. Don't be afraid to tell God how you feel, but also include praise for who He is and all that He has done and is going to do in your life.

PSALM 103 – DAY 1

Praise The Lord!

Let all that I am praise the Lord; may I never forget the good things he does for me. – Psalm 103:2 NLT

Gratefulness to God begins with an awareness of all that He has done for us. Failure to recognize God's activity in our lives makes it extremely unlikely that we will be grateful. It's hard to praise Him for all that He has done for us if we don't recognize it to begin with. In this psalm, David seems to be reminding himself of God's daily activities in his life. He even says, "May I never forget the good things he does for me" (Psalm 103:2b NLT). Then he goes on to list all those "good things:"

- He forgives all my sins
- He heals all my diseases
- He redeems me from death
- He crowns me with love and tender mercies
- He fills my life with good things
- He renews my youth
- He gives righteousness and justice
- He is compassionate and merciful
- He is slow to get angry
- He is filled with unfailing love
- He will not constantly accuse us
- He doesn't remain angry with us forever
- He doesn't punish us for all our sins
- He doesn't deal harshly with us, as we deserve
- He shows us unfailing love that is immeasurable and unlimited
- He has removed our sins as for as the east is from the west
- He treats us like a father would his children
- He is tender and compassionate
- He knows and understands our weaknesses
- His love for us remains forever

- He rules over everything

That's a pretty extensive list, and it is not unique to David. Every single one of these "good things" are available to us as His children. They are just as true of my relationship with God as they were of David. The problem is that we don't tend to think about them. Instead, we dwell on all those things we believe God has failed to do for us. We concentrate on what we believe to be are unanswered prayers and unmet expectations. We may have some specific need we want addressed and, in our estimation, God has failed to deal with it adequately. In the meantime, we fail to recognize and appreciate His unfailing love, mercy, forgiveness, and grace that He extends to us day after day – like clockwork.

One of the most amazing realizations David expresses in this psalm is found in verse 10. The *NET Bible* translates it this way: "He does not deal with us as our sins deserve; he does not repay us as our misdeeds deserve."[17] This is another way of looking at God's incredible mercy and grace. You see, mercy is God *not* giving you what you deserve (withheld punishment), and grace is God giving you what you *don't* deserve (unmerited favor). David understood that God had every right as God to deal with him harshly due to the sin in his life, but He chose to show mercy instead. Rather than give us what we deserve, God gives us what we don't deserve – His grace. Until we come to grips with the reality of that statement, we will never truly praise God for who He is and what He has done. Christ's death on the cross is the ultimate expression of God's love and grace. His death made possible our forgiveness. His sacrifice allowed God to withhold our punishment because, in taking our place and dying on our behalf, Christ paid our debt in full. The righteous wrath of God was satisfied once and for all. As a result, God has removed our sins as far from us as the east is from the west. We no longer stand before God as guilty and condemned, but as forgiven and redeemed. He sees us as righteous and holy.

So if we think about it, we have just as much to be grateful for as David did – even more. We have enjoyed the benefit of Christ's sacrificial, substitutionary death on the cross. So, like David, we should be able to say, "Let all that I am praise the Lord; with my whole heart, I will praise his holy name" (Psalm 103:1 NLT).

---

[17] *NET Bible*, Biblical Studies Press, L.L.C., http://netbible.com

Father, the good things You have done for me are real and deserving of my gratitude and praise. I should be praising You for who You are and all that You have done and continue to do on a daily basis. Open my eyes and help me see Your activity in and around my life. Give me an increasing awareness of Your grace and mercy so that I will praise You more. Amen

PSALM 103 – DAY 2

Plenty of Reasons To Praise Him.
Based on Psalm 103

I will bless the Lord from the depths of my very being.
I will praise Him for His matchless reputation.
I will bless Him and not forget all He has done for me.
He forgives all my sins and heals me when I am sick.
He pays my way out of the pit, and crowns me with love and compassion,
He provides me with good things to eat and renews my strength so that I
*   fly high like an eagle,*
The Lord always does what is righteous and provides justice for the oppressed.
Moses got to experience the character of God, so did the people of Israel.
They discovered that the Lord is compassionate, gracious, patient and never
*   runs out of mercy.*
He will not always accuse us of our sins or remain angry with us forever,
He hasn't done to us what we deserved or rewarded us in keeping with our sins.
No, He has shown unimaginable, unlimited mercy to those of us who fear Him.
He has removed the guilt of our sins from us as far as the east is from the west.
He shows compassion on those who hear Him like a father does for his children.
He knows us well and understands that we have about as much value as dust.
To God, our lifetimes are like grass. We have the lifespan of a flower in a field.
It dies and the wind blows it away. And with it, the memory that it ever even existed.

But the Lord constantly and consistently shows mercy to those who fear Him,
And the generations that follow them get to experience His righteousness –
As long as they keep His covenants and obey His commands.
The Lord reigns on His throne from heaven and rules over everything and everyone.
Even angels, in all their supernatural strength, praise the Lord, obeying His commands
And doing everything that He says.
Praise Him, all who are His warriors, carrying out His desires.
Let everything and everyone He has made in every sphere of His kingdom praise Him!

PSALM 103 – DAY 3

Write Psalm 103 in your own words or write a psalm of your own. Be honest and open. Don't be afraid to tell God how you feel, but also include praise for who He is and all that He has done and is going to do in your life.

PSALM 108 – DAY 1

Well-Placed Confidence.

My heart is confident in you, O God; no wonder I can sing your praises with all my heart. – Psalm 108:1 NLT

David is ready. He is prepared to face anything. He is strong and confident. Why? Because of God. This is not a case of self-confidence or self-sufficiency. David is confessing that his hope and trust are in God alone. He knows that with God's help he can face any situation with confidence and peace. He says, "With God's help we will do mighty things, for he will trample down our foes" (Psalm 108:13 NLT). There is no enemy too powerful or problem too big for God. David has learned that fearing is futile and pointless when God is on your side. Trying to take matters into your own hands is ridiculous when you have the God of the universe fighting for you. David's awareness of this fact causes him to sing God's praises. He can't help but express gratefulness for God's unfailing love and faithfulness. He has seen it in the past and he is confident that he will see it again in the future, all because of what he knows about God's unchanging nature. God has promised to rescue His people "by His holiness" (Psalm 108:7 NLT). His very character assures that He will do what He has promised to do. He will come through. He will answer.

But in the midst of the storm it is easy to forget that God is faithful. When surrounded by trouble, it is tempting to doubt that God will keep His promises. Like David, we can begin to question God, "Have you rejected us, O God" Will you no longer march with our armies?" (Psalm 108:11 NLT). It is during those times we must remind ourselves that God is faithful. He rescues. He restores. He may not do it according to our schedule or exactly as we would like it done, but He will do it. The temptation for us during those seasons of apparent inaction on God's part, is to turn to someone or something else for help. In many cases, we are tempted to trust ourselves for the solution we're looking for, in spite of our own abysmal track record. But David knew better. He said, "all human help is useless" (Psalm 108:12b NLT). Anything we turn to as a substitute for

God will eventually fail us. But with God's help we will do mighty things. This is a lesson only learned through experience. It can be taught, but it is rarely caught, until we are forced to experience it first hand. Relying on God takes guts. Trusting Him when everything in you says to take matters into your own hands takes faith. But as we grow in our understanding of His character, we become increasingly more confident and quick to place our trust in Him and Him alone.

Father, continue to teach me to trust You. Thank You that my heart is more confident in You today than it has ever been. I still have a long way to go, but You have never given me a reason to doubt You. Amen

PSALM 108 – DAY 2

Ready For Anything.
Based on Psalm 108

O God, my heart is stable and secure in You,
I will sing Your praises with everything in me.
Wake up, musical instruments! Help me welcome the day with music.
I will praise You among my own people and in front of the nations.
All because Your mercy is as high as the heavens,
And Your faithfulness extends to the clouds.
Magnify Yourself all the way to heaven,
And let Your glory be seen above the earth.
Answer my prayer by delivering those You love with mercy and faithfulness,
Save them with Your powerful right hand.
You have made Your promises based on Your holiness,
"I will rejoice in triumph, dividing up Shechem,
And measuring out the valley of Succoth.
Gilead and Manasseh are mine, Ephraim is my helmet, Judah my scepter,
Moab is my washbasin, Edom is where I will throw my dirty sandal.
I will stand in triumph over Philistia."
So who will make it possible for me to enter the fortified city?
Who will lead me in victory into Edom?
Aren't You the one who has rejected us, O God?
Are You not going to go into battle with our army?
Grant us assistance against our enemies,
For the deliverance of men is worthless.
Only You, O God, allow our army to appear powerful,
Because it is You who really brings about the victory, not us.

PSALM 108 – DAY 3

Write Psalm 108 in your own words or write a psalm of your own. Be honest and open. Don't be afraid to tell God how you feel, but also include praise for who He is and all that He has done and is going to do in your life.

PSALM 109 – DAY 1

When All Else Fails – God Won't.

But deal well with me, O Sovereign Lord, for the sake of your own reputation! Rescue me because you are so faithful and good. – Psalm 109:21 NLT

David has some real classy friends. He loves and prays for them, and in return, they slander him, tell lies about him, falsely accuse him, and wish all kinds of bad things would happen to him, including death and the impoverishment of his children. As the old saying goes, with friends like that, who needs enemies? These people, whoever they are, have it out for David, and they are calling down the judgment of God on him. David is misunderstood, mistreated, disliked, and disdained by his so-called friends. So he does the one thing he knows to do in tough times – he calls on God. He appeals to the only one who can do anything about his situation. And he bases his appeal to God on His reputation for holiness, righteousness, justice and equity. He knows that God understands the situation better than anyone else, and that God is the only one who can do anything about it. God is fully aware of the accusations leveled against David and He knows whether they are true or not. David doesn't have to defend himself to God, because God already knows the truth. David calls out to God because he is poor and needy and his heart is full of pain (Psalm 109:22). He claims, "I am fading like a shadow at dusk; I am brushed off like a locust. My knees are weak from fasting, and I am skin and bones. I am a joke to people everywhere; when they see me, they shake their heads in scorn" (Psalm 109:22-25 NLT). David is in a bad spot. He is under attack and overwhelmed by his circumstances, so he cries out to God. He appeals to His mercy, grace, righteousness, goodness, and unfailing love. He knows that if God is on His side, it doesn't matter what his "friends" say or do to him. "Then let them curse me if they like, but you will bless me!" (Psalm 109:28 NLT). David knows that God will deal favorably with him. He will rescue and restore him. God will give David plenty of reasons to praise Him when it is all said and done. "I will give repeated thanks to the Lord, praising him to everyone. For he stands beside the needy, ready to save them from those who condemn them" (Psalm 109:30-31 NLT). While everything seemed to be failing around David, he knew his God would not let him down. He knew God to be faithful, true, reliable, and always ready to stand by those He loves. Friends may desert and disappoint us, but God never will. When all else fails, God won't.

Father, sometimes in the midst of difficulty it is easy to lose sight of the fact that You are faithful – all the time. I can easily begin to think that You have left me and forsaken me. But You are faithful. Your love is not fickle or fluctuating. Your character is always consistent. When everything and everyone else fails me, You never will. Thank You! Amen

PSALM 109 – DAY 2

Bad Times. Good Times.
Based on Psalm 109

O God, You are one the one I praise.
Now I need to hear from You, for you to break Your silence.
The wicked and deceivers have no trouble speaking up,
They slander me and tell lies about me all the time.
I am surrounded by their hateful words,
And they oppose me for no reason.
I show them love and they respond with accusations.
But I continue to pray for them.
I do them good, and I get evil in return.
I get hatred as payback for my love.
This is what they have to say about me:
"Let's get a someone to accuse him falsely,
Someone who can take him to court under false pretenses.
Then when his case comes up for trial, let's hope he loses.
May even his prayers be viewed as sin when this is over.
We wish him a short life, so someone else can have his job.
Let his kids end up fatherless and his wife a widow!
May his kids become homeless beggars, searching for food in the dump.
May his creditors take all he owns, and strangers end up with the rest.
May he have no future and leave no legacy.
May God remember his sins forever and punish his family accordingly.
He is a merciless man who refuses to care for the poor and needy,
He took advantage of the down-trodden.
He loved to curse others, so let him be cursed,
Since he refused to bless others, don't let him experience it.
He clothed himself in a life of cursing and it has seeped into his own life,
Let curses surround him like the fancy clothes he wears."

But Lord, I ask that You turn these curses back on my adversaries,
I ask You to treat me according to Your reputation. Show me mercy. Rescue me.
I am poor, needy, and suffer from a broken heart.

I am fading quickly and blown back and forth like a helpless insect.
I am weak from fasting and I have no energy left.
Everyone looks at me with either pity or disgust, shaking their heads.
Help me, O God, answer me according to Your mercy!
May they be able to see that it was You who rescued me.
Let them curse, but You bless.

When they rise up against me, let them be disappointed and let me rejoice.
May they wear their shame and confusion like a cheap suit.
When You act, I will praise You, O Lord, I will praise You among the people.
You stand by those in need, and deliver them from those who oppose them.

PSALM 109 – DAY 3

Write Psalm 109 in your own words or write a psalm of your own. Be honest and open. Don't be afraid to tell God how you feel, but also include praise for who He is and all that He has done and is going to do in your life.

PSALMS 110 – DAY 1

The Ultimate David.

The LORD said to my Lord, "Sit in the place of honor at my right hand until I humble your enemies, making them a footstool under your feet." – Psalm 110:1 NLT

This is a somewhat confusing psalm. It was written by David, but he appears to be talking about someone else. The term, Lord, is mentioned twice, but it seems a bit unclear as to whom David is referring. Is David talking about himself or someone else? Are all the statements in this passage referring to him or another person? In the Hebrew culture, the term, *The Lord*, was understood to be a reference to the Messiah, the coming Savior of Israel. So in the psalm, David is referring not to himself, but to the future Messiah, God's divinely appointed ruler over Israel. This psalm is a prophesy regarding Jesus and His coming role as the conquering Messiah that will take place at the end of the ages. David knew there was a day coming when all the enemies of Israel would be completely destroyed by the King of kings and Lord of Lords – Jesus the Christ or Messiah. Over in the book of Matthew we have recorded an incident between Jesus and the Pharisees, where Jesus used this very passage to point to himself.

> *While the Pharisees were assembled, Jesus asked them a question: "What do you think about the Christ? Whose son is he?" They said, "The son of David." He said to them, "How then does David by the Spirit call him 'Lord,' saying, 'The Lord said to my lord, "Sit at my right hand, until I put your enemies under your feet"? If David then calls him 'Lord,' how can he be his son?" No one was able to answer him a word, and from that day on no one dared to question him any longer.* – Matthew 22:41-46 NLT

Jesus knew that this psalm was a prediction of an event that had not yet taken place. It was still unfulfilled, but would take place somewhere in the future. But there was no doubt in Jesus' mind that Psalm 110 was talking about Him. And it is a reminder to us that there is a day coming when Jesus, as the Christ (the Greek word for Messiah), will return to the earth to complete the plan of God for Israel and all mankind. Jesus' work is not yet done. At this very moment He sits at the right hand of the Father in heaven, but when God is ready, He will send Jesus to "strike down many kings when his anger erupts. He will punish the nations and fill their land with corpses; he will shatter heads over the whole earth. But he himself will be refreshed from brooks along the way. He will be victorious" (Psalm 110:5-7 NLT).

For David, a king, this was a wonderful picture of victory over his enemies. He knew that someday God was going to give Israel complete victory over every one of their foes. David lived in a time when battle was a daily ordeal. He was surrounded by enemies and regularly confronted by war. There was never a day when someone didn't want to destroy him or the nation over which he ruled. So the idea of final victory and an end to all wars was appealing to him. And it should be to us as well. Like David, we are surrounded by enemies, by those who oppose God and His ways. They live for this world and are influenced by the Prince of this world, Satan himself. Everyday we go to war with our own flesh, the world and the ruler of this world. We are under constant attack. There is never a time when we can take a day off or remove our armor. We must be constantly prepared to defend ourselves. The war is real and so are the casualties. We see them in the form of broken marriages, rebellious kids, addictions of all kinds, depression, anxiety, and an assortment of diseases. This psalm assures us that there is a day coming when God will set all things right. His plan will be finalized. His Son, the Messiah, will finish what He came to do. His first coming provided a way of salvation for mankind. He made it possible for us to be made right with God. He offered all mankind a means by which they could escape the coming wrath of God against all who refuse Him. But there is a day coming when Christ will return, but this time it will not be as Savior, but as a conquering King. He will do battle with all those who stand against God and He will be victorious. The enemy will be defeated once and for all. He will set up His kingdom on earth and He will rule from Jerusalem. There will be peace in the world for the first time since the creation of the world. Order will be restored, shalom will be present once more. He will be victorious.

Father, in the midst of the daily battles of life it is so easy to get defeated by what appears to be a hopeless cause. It can be so easy to want to give up and give in. Our efforts seem to make no difference. The battles we fight don't seem to be winning the war. But in this psalm You remind us that the ultimate victory is Yours, not ours. David had to fight his battles, but he rested in the knowledge that You were going to one day bring about complete victory. Don't let me forget that. Amen

PSALM 110 – DAY 2

The Messiah.
Based on Psalm 110

God said to my LORD, *the Messiah,*
"Sit at the place of honor at my right side, until I put all Your enemies under your feet."
God will stretch out the rod representing Your strength from Zion.
He will command You to rule over all of your enemies.
When that happens, all Your people will gladly follow You.
When the day dawns, You will show up in all Your holiness
*   and with the strength of youth.*
God has made a vow and will not change His mind,
You will be a permanent priest after the order of Melchizedek.
When You get ready to deal out Your wrath on the nations,
You will use Him who sits at Your right hand,
He will execute Your judgment among the nations,
He will punish them for their sins, leaving corpses in His wake.
He will shatter the heads of the nations.
He will refresh Himself at the brook along the way,
And complete His task with head held high!

PSALM 110 – DAY 3

Write Psalm 110 in your own words or write a psalm of your own. Be honest and open. Don't be afraid to tell God how you feel, but also include praise for who He is and all that He has done and is going to do in your life.

PSALMS 122, 124 – DAY 1

A Question Worth Asking.

What if the Lord had not been on our side? – Psalm 124:1a NLT

What if the Lord had not been on our side? What if He had not answered our prayers? What if He had refused to rescue us? What if He had not sent His Son to die in our place? These are all sobering questions that require us to consider **not** the consequences if our God ever failed to come through, but the reality that He always does. He is always faithful and true. He is always on our side. It may not appear like it at times, but His very nature, His character, assures us that He is for us and not against us.

These two psalms are part of a collection of psalms called the Songs of Ascent. They were sung by the pilgrims making their annual journey to Jerusalem for Pentecost and the Feast of Tabernacles, both celebrations associated with the Passover. These songs were sung along the way, reminding the travelers of their destination and the One for whom they were making this long arduous journey in order to worship Him. They were going to Jerusalem "to give thanks to the name of the Lord, as the law requires of Israel" (Psalm 122:4b NLT). The name of the Lord was synonymous with His reputation. He was…

El Shaddai (Lord God Almighty),
El Elyon (The Most High God),
Adonai (Lord, Master),
Jehovah Nissi (The Lord My Banner),
Jehovah-Raah (The Lord My Shephard),
Jehovah Rapha (The Lord That Heals),
Jehovah Shammah (The Lord Is There),
Jehovah Tsidkenu (The Lord Our Righteousness),
Jehovah Mekoddishkem (The Lord Who Sanctifies You),
El Olam (The Everlasting God),
Jehovah Jireh (The Lord Will Provide),
Jehovah Shalom (The Lord Is Peace), and

Jehovah Sabaoth (The Lord Of Hosts).

These names of God represent a picture of who He is and all that He had done for the people of Israel. They went up each year as a nation to celebrate all His attributes and to thank Him for the actions He had accomplished on their behalf.

But they also celebrated the reality that, without God, they would have no hope. Had God not been on their side, "The waters would have engulfed us; a torrent would have overwhelmed us" (Psalm 124:4 NLT). They recognized that life without God would have been no life at all. They understood that their help was from the Lord, the same Creator God who had made heaven and earth. This all-powerful God had chosen to have a personal relationship with them and provide them with His protection, provision and ongoing presence. But rather than take this fact for granted, the people of Israel reminded themselves what life would be like if things were different. They asked the sobering question, "What if the Lord had not been on our side?" We could probably stand to do the same thing. Sometimes it makes sense to consider what life would be like without God in order to truly appreciate all that we enjoy because of Him.

Father, my life is nothing without You. My future would be hopeless without You. My life would have no meaning apart from You. But because of who You are, I know I have help, hope, and healing at my disposal. I have a relationship with the God of the universe. Thank You. Amen

PSALMS 122, 124 – DAY 2

A Love For God's House.
Based on Psalm 122

I was overjoyed when I heard the news that it was time to head to God's house.
We were going to get to stand within the very gates of Jerusalem.
Jerusalem was established as a city to unify the people of God by bringing them together.
It is where all the tribes of Israel gather to keep their promise to worship God,
To show gratitude for His reputation as their God.
There in Jerusalem are thrones of judgment, including the throne of the house of David.
We need to pray for the peace, welfare and prosperity of Jerusalem,
Because as long as Jerusalem prospers, so will all those who love this city.
We pray for peace to exist throughout the city, inside its walls and its palaces,
For the sake of my fellow Israelites, I say, "May there be peace in Jerusalem!"
Because the house of God is there, I will seek the good of Jerusalem.

God Is On Our Side.
Based on Psalm 124

Let us remind ourselves, "What if God had not been on our side?"
May all of Israel say, "What if God had not been on our side when our enemies rose up
* against us?"*
We would have easily been defeated by them when they turned their anger against us.
We would have been overwhelmed, our souls would have been drowned.
The raging waters would have flooded over our soul.
But let us kneel before God, who didn't let any of that happen,
He helped us escape, like a bird from a trap set by a hunter.
God broke the snare and we escaped.
We find help in the reputation of the Lord, the one who made heaven and earth.

PSALMS 122, 124 – DAY 3

Write Psalm 122 in your own words or write a psalm of your own. Be honest and open. Don't be afraid to tell God how you feel, but also include praise for who He is and all that He has done and is going to do in your life.

PSALMS 122, 124 – DAY 3

Write Psalm 124 in your own words or write a psalm of your own. Be honest and open. Don't be afraid to tell God how you feel, but also include praise for who He is and all that He has done and is going to do in your life.

PSALMS 131, 133 – DAY 1

The Beauty of Unity.

How wonderful and pleasant it is when brothers lives together in harmony! – Psalm 133:1 NLT

These two psalms are also part of the Songs of Ascent, a collection of psalms that were sung as pilgrims made their annual journey to Jerusalem for the celebration of Passover. Psalm 131 places the emphasis on the individual. In it, David expresses his humility. He doesn't think too highly of himself. He refuses to think of himself as too smart for his own good or better than anyone else – in spite of the fact that he is the king. In Psalm 133, he turns his attention to the communal aspect of his faith. He recognizes that he is part of a collection of individuals who together make up the family of God. But it is about more than community, it is about harmony and unity. This is to be true of the church as well. In his letter to the Philippian church, Paul writes, "Is there any encouragement from belonging to Christ? Any comfort from his love? Any fellowship together in the Spirit? Are your hearts tender and compassionate? Then make me truly happy by agreeing wholeheartedly with each other, loving one another, and working together with one mind and purpose. Don't be selfish; don't try to impress others. Be humble, thinking of others as better than yourselves. Don't look out only for your own interests, but take an interest in others, too. You must have the same attitude that Christ Jesus had" (Philippians 2:1-5 NLT). He then goes on to describe the attitude that Christ had: One of humility, service, sacrifice, love, and obedience. Paul says that we are to have this same mindset. We are to pursue unity through humility.

Paul stresses the same idea in his letter to the Ephesian church: "Therefore I, a prisoner for serving the Lord, beg you to lead a life worthy of your calling, for you have been called by God. Always be humble and gentle. Be patient with each other, making allowance for each other's faults because of your love. Make every effort to keep yourselves united in the Spirit, binding yourselves together with peace" (Ephesians 4:1-3 NLT). There it is again.

Humility. Unity. Oneness. Paul saw the wisdom in what David had written hundreds of years earlier. It truly is wonderful and pleasant when brothers live together in harmony. And because of what Christ accomplished on the cross and due to the influence of the indwelling Holy Spirit, we have the capacity to love as no one has ever loved before. We have the mind of Christ and can love as He loved, sacrifice in the same way, humble ourselves as He did, and give our lives away in selfless service to others. Especially within the context of the body of Christ.

Before He went to His death on the cross, Jesus spoke these words to His disciples: "So now I am giving you a new commandment: Love each other. Just as I have loved you, you should love each other. Your love for one another will prove to the world that you are my disciples" (John 13:34-35 NLT). Jesus commanded His followers to love one another. That would be the distinguishing characteristic to prove that we belonged to Him. It would demonstrate our relationship with Him. It is amazing how much emphasis we put on the Great Commission, feeling the need to go out into the world and make disciples. But we rarely, if ever, talk about this command from the lips of Jesus. He is calling us to love for one another – those within the body of Christ, the church. He is commanding us to love as He loved – to the point of death. But is that really happening? Does the world know we are His disciples because of our selfless love for one another, or because of our acts of charity, our generosity, our missions endeavors, our ability to share the Gospel, or our organization effectiveness? Are the lost attracted to our love for one another? Do they see in us something they can't see anywhere else in the world? Christ has given us the capacity to love and be loved. He has created a new thing called the church, the family of God. In it, we are to live out the character of Christ in the context of community. What good is it to express our love for the lost when we have a hard time loving one another? How wonderful and pleasant it is when brothers and sisters live together in harmony!

Father, as the church, we have failed to obey the command of Your own Son. We do not love one another as He has called us to love. We can be petty, selfish, divisive, competitive, and mean. We can attempt to do great things for Your kingdom while we refuse to love one another as we have been loved by You. Open our eyes and help us to understand that the church is a noun, not a verb. We are Your people. We are to live as such. We are Your children. We are to get along. We represent You in the world. But if we can't love one another, the Good News loses much of its power. Amen

PSALMS 131, 133 – DAY 2

It's Not All About Me.
Based on Psalm 131

Lord, I don't have an arrogant heart,
I don't look down on others as if I'm better than they are.
I don't walk around with an attitude of self-importance,
Or as if I am somehow God's gift to the world.
I am calm and quiet, weaned off my incessant need for significance,
Like a baby gets weaned off its mothers milk.
So Israel, put your hope in the Lord and not me, from this point forward!

It's All About Us.
Based on Psalm 133

How wonderful and delightful it is to live our lives alongside one another!
This sense of togetherness is pervasive, like the oil used to anoint Aaron,
It ran from his head to his beard and all the way to the bottom of his robe.
It is like the dew that falls on Mount Hermon, that covers the mountains of Zion,
For it was there that God promised His blessing to us as His people,
Life in the community of God that will never end.

PSALM S 131, 133 – DAY 3

Write Psalm 131 in your own words or write a psalm of your own. Be honest and open. Don't be afraid to tell God how you feel, but also include praise for who He is and all that He has done and is going to do in your life.

PSALMS 131, 133 – DAY 3

Write Psalm 133 in your own words or write a psalm of your own. Be honest and open. Don't be afraid to tell God how you feel, but also include praise for who He is and all that He has done and is going to do in your life.

PSALMS 138-139 – DAY 1

Nobody Knows Me Better.

The Lord will work out his plans for my life – for your faithful love, O Lord, endures forever. – Psalm 138:8 NLT

There are times when I don't even know myself. I do and say things that surprise even me. I can never know for sure how I will react to a given situation. I may respond in calmness and patience one day, then explode in anger and impatience the next. I have a limited understanding of what motivates me and why I act the way I do. Sometimes words come out of my mouth that catch me off guard. I can be disappointed in my own response to people and circumstances. There are those moments when I can appear as a stranger – even to myself.

But God knows me. He knows me better than I know myself. David understood this unbelievable characteristic about God. He knew that God was all-knowing, all-powerful, and always present. He knew that God was always there, and that God knew every single detail of his life, including what he was thinking and what he was going to say, even before the words came out of his mouth. David also understood that God had a plan for his life and that He was working that plan each and every day – regardless of how David's circumstances may have appeared. All of this news about God can be both encouraging and scary. The fact that God knows everything there is to know about us can be a bit intimidating, or we can find it comforting. David was prone to the latter. He understood that along with God's divine attributes of omniscience (He knows everything), omnipotence (He is all-powerful), and omnipresence (He is everywhere at once), God was also all-loving, completely faithful, and a God who keeps all of His promises all of the time. So the fact that God knew all of David's thoughts didn't scare him, it comforted him. David was able to say, "O Lord, you have examined my heart and know everything about me" (Psalm 139:1 NLT). That thought caused David to say, "Such knowledge is too wonderful for me, too great for me to understand" (Psalm 139:6 NLT). David might not have fully comprehended the reality of God's all-knowing, all-powerful presence in his life, but he **did** appreciate it. David knew that God had created him – he was a byproduct of God's imagination and creative capabilities. He was not a mistake or an act of chance. "You saw me before I was born. Every day of my life was recorded in your book. Every moment was laid out before a single day had passed" (Psalm 139:16 NLT). What an amazing thought.

This understanding of God's intimate relationship with him caused David to invite God to do something that for many of us sounds a bit risky. It comes across like an invitation that could end up producing some less-than-satisfactory results. But keep in mind, David knew that God loved him and had a plan for his life. He trusted God. There was nothing that God did not know about his life. There was nothing that David thought or did that was hidden from God. So he asked God to "Search me, O God, and know my heart; test me and know my anxious thoughts. Point out anything in me that offends you, and lead me along the path of everlasting life" (Psalm 1139:23-24 NLT). David was asking God to reveal to him what only God knew about him. David was asking God to show him things about his life he was incapable of seeing or even knowing. As human beings, we can't really know our hearts. We can't fully understand our motives. We are blinded by pride and self-righteousness, and we can deceive ourselves into thinking we are really better than we are. So David goes to the one source that can see past the facade and look into the inner recesses of his heart. He asks God, the all-knowing, all-seeing, all-loving God to do an MRI of his life and reveal the results. David knew that God loved him and had a plan for his life. But David also knew that he was a man who was prone to sin. He knew his heart was not to be trusted. He was painfully aware that he was incapable of really knowing what was going on in his heart. So he asked God to examine, test, and prove him. He asked God to point out anything and everything that was an offense to Him. Scary? Yes. Risky? Not really. David was simply asking to learn what God already knew. David was tapping into God's limitless understanding and relying on God's unfailing love for him.

Father, You love me. And what's amazing is that You love me even though You know everything there is to know about me. There is nothing I can hide from You. I can't fool you with my pious activities or acts of religious pretense. I can't fake faith in front of You. You know me just as I am and yet You love me anyway. Give me the heart of David, that I might be willing to ask You to search me, test me, know the cause of all my anxious thoughts, and point out everything in my life that offends You. The sooner I see the truth about myself, the sooner I can confess my sins and get back on Your path for my life. Amen

PSALMS 138-139 – DAY 2

God Has A Plan For My Life.
Based on Psalm 138

I want to thank You from the depths of my heart.
I will sing Your praises so even the angels in heaven can hear me!
I will bow toward Your holy temple in Jerusalem and offer thanks for Your reputation:
Your unfailing love and faithfulness.
And keeping Your word is the greatest aspect of Your reputation.
Any time I have ever called out to You for help, You have always answered.
As a result I was filled with a boldness and confidence inside.
Every powerful person on earth would praise You, if they ever stopped long enough to
*   listen to You.*
And some day they will praise You, because You are an incredible God.
Yet even though You are exalted, You take time to care about the down and out.
But You keep Your distance from the proud.
And even though I live my life surrounded by trouble,
You keep me alive, opposing all my enemies, and protecting me in Your hand.
You will complete Your plan for my life, because Your love for me never does fail.
You don't abandon those whom You have made.

You Know Me Better Than I Know Myself.
Based on Psalm 139

O Lord, You have examined me closely and know everything there is to know about me.
You know every time I sit and every time I stand up.
Distance doesn't prevent You from understanding every one of my thoughts.
Nothing I do escapes You, whether I am out and about or in bed.
You are highly familiar with everything I do.
You know what I am going to say before I even have a chance to say it!
You know my past and my future, Your hand is all over me.
When I think about all this, it blows me away, I can't even comprehend it all.
Where can I go to escape You, or even attempt to hide from You?
If I were able to go to heaven, You would be there.
If I went the opposite direction, You would be there too.
If I got up at dawn and went to the other side of the sea,
You would still be guiding me and holding me in Your hand!
Even if I thought I could hide from Your view at night,
You would see me just as clearly, because day and night are one and the same to You.
You have been in control of my life from the beginning, from before I was even born.
I will praise You because You made me and that knowledge inspires both fear and
        wonder.
Nothing about me was unknown to You when I was formed,
You saw me even in my unfinished state,
You had recorded every day of my life before I had even lived a single second.
How priceless are your plans for me, O Lord, I can't even add up their value.
Even if I could try to count them, they would be like the sand on the seashore!
Every time I wake up, I find myself in Your presence.
You will take care of the wicked people in my life, so they might as well leave now.
These people actually treat You wickedly, using Your name in vain.
I hate them because they hate You. I am burdened by those who resist You.
I despise them and count them as my enemies.
But I invite You to examine me, O Lord, to perceive what is in my heart;
Test me and know the content of my thoughts.
Inspect me closely, and see if there is anything about the way I live my life that is wrong,
And lead me along the path of righteousness You have chosen for me.

PSALMS 138-139 – DAY 3

Write Psalm 138 in your own words or write a psalm of your own. Be honest and open. Don't be afraid to tell God how you feel, but also include praise for who He is and all that He has done and is going to do in your life.

PSALMS 138-139 – DAY 3

Write Psalm 139 in your own words or write a psalm of your own. Be honest and open. Don't be afraid to tell God how you feel, but also include praise for who He is and all that He has done and is going to do in your life.

PSALMS 140-142 – DAY 1

Seeing God As God.

I said to the LORD, *"You are my God!"* – Psalm 140:6 NLT

What an interesting statement. "I said to the Lord, 'You are my God!'" Did God need to be told this? Was this some kind of revelation to Him from the lips of David? I don't think so. But it was David's way of saying that Jehovah (LORD), was the one he turned to, relied on, and believed in. David proved it by the content of the three prayers reflected by these three psalms. David turns to God for rescue, protection, mercy, vengeance, justice, motivation for righteousness, help in times of trouble, refuge, compassion, empathy, understanding, encouragement, and strength. In fact, David knew he could turn to God when everyone else had proven themselves unreliable, unresponsive and uncaring. "I look for someone to come and help me, but no one gives me a passing thought! No one will help me; no one cares a bit what happens to me. Then, I pray to you, O Lord" (Psalm 142:4-5 NLT).

To say that the Lord is my God is to say that He is my sole source of hope and the only object of my faith. I don't have any other gods before me. I don't worship anything or anyone else. I don't turn to anything else for comfort or security, including fame, fortune, or friendships. To say that God is my God is to claim exclusive worship. It is to promise God that He alone is my Savior. He alone can rescue me. Only He can do something about my problems, which usually have far more to do with my own heart than my circumstances. To tell God that He is my God is a form of confession, but also a statement of commitment. Like David, I am saying that my allegiance belongs to Him, my prayers are directed to Him, my hope is placed in Him, and my worship is reserved for Him – and Him alone.

These three psalms are expressions of need. They clearly indicate David's hurt and heartache. David is opening up his soul to his God. He is telling Him exactly how he feels, because he knows that God cares and that God can do something about it. Every time we pray to God, we prove to Him that He is our God. We acknowledge our dependence on Him. Our prayers become "as incense offered" and our "upraised hands as an evening offering." God truly becomes our God when we rest in Him, rely on Him, turn to Him, and trust in Him.

Father, You are my God. You alone hear my prayers and have the capacity to answer them. You can do something about my needs and love me enough to do so. But I confess there are plenty of times I turn to other things for comfort, help, hope, security, and salvation. Thank You for Your patience with me. Continue to help me discover the truth of the statement, "You are my God!" Amen

PSALMS 140-142 – DAY 2

You Are My God.
Based on Psalm 140

Save me, O Lord, from the evil person.
Faithfully keep me from the man who does wrong,
Whose heart is constantly plotting to do evil,
And lives to stir up trouble.
Their tongue pierces like the fangs of a snake,
Their smooth talk conceals poison.
Watch over me and protect me, O Lord, from the hands of the wicked.
Act as a watchman, guarding me from the violent man,
Who is out to knock me down with every step I take.
These arrogant individuals secretly lay traps for me,
They lay a net along the path, using bait to lure me in.
I said to the Lord, "You are my God!"
Listen to my pleas for help!
You are Jehovah Adonai, the one whose strength provides my salvation.
You watched over me in battle, covering me with Your hand.
Don't let the wicked have their way, O Lord,
Don't let their wicked plans succeed, because they are proud.
As for the ringleader of the group who surrounds me,
Let the plans they have to harm me come back on them.
Let them get burned by their own wicked schemes,
Burn them with fire and let them fall into a deep pit from which they can't escape.
Don't let these men who slander others survive on this earth,
Let evil pursue them and overthrow them.
I know from experience that You will protect those whom they persecute,
You will show justice to those who deserve it.
Surely the righteous will have plenty of reason to praise Your name,
Those who live to please You will enjoy being in Your presence.

I Look To You For Help!
Based on Psalm 141

Lord, I call out to You, respond to me quickly!
Listen to the sound of my voice as I call out to You!
Let my prayer to You be a sweet fragrance to You, like incense,
And my uplifted hands like an acceptable sacrifice.
Guard my speech, O Lord, watch over what I say,
Don't allow my heart to pursue evil,
Don't let me follow the example of those who do wrong,
Or consume the "tasty treats" they offer.
Let the godly beat me into shape like a blacksmith does metal, out of love for me.
Let me find their correction soothing and healing,
But I will continue to pray against the wicked and all that they do.
Even their judges will be judged and thrown off the cliff to their deaths,
Then they will listen to all I have said and know I was right.
Our bones got scattered before we had a chance for burial,
We lie out in the open like rocks stirred up by the plow.
So I look to You, O Lord, it is in You I place my trust.
Don't disappoint me!
Guard me from falling into the trap they have set for me,
And don't let me take the bait they offer.
Instead, let them fall into their own traps and let me escape.

You Know What I Should Do.
Based on Psalm 142

I cry out to You, O Lord, I call out to You for mercy.
I spill my guts to You, I let You know all of my troubles.
But right when I felt like all was lost, You knew exactly where I was,
You were completely aware of all the traps they had set for me,
From my perspective, I looked around and their was no one to help me,
No one to understand what I was going through, and nobody offering to help.
There was no one who even really cared.
So I cried out to You, O Lord,
I said, "You are my refuge, the only thing I really need in this life!"
Hear my cry, because I am at a really low point,
Deliver me from those who persecute me, because they are stronger than I am.
Release me from this prison, so that I can have reason to praise Your name,
Bring me into the company of other godly people, so they can support me.

PSALMS 140-142 – DAY 3

Write Psalm 140 in your own words or write a psalm of your own. Be honest and open. Don't be afraid to tell God how you feel, but also include praise for who He is and all that He has done and is going to do in your life.

PSALMS 140-142 – DAY 3

Write Psalm 141 in your own words or write a psalm of your own. Be honest and open. Don't be afraid to tell God how you feel, but also include praise for who He is and all that He has done and is going to do in your life.

PSALMS 140-142 – DAY 3

Write Psalm 142 in your own words or write a psalm of your own. Be honest and open. Don't be afraid to tell God how you feel, but also include praise for who He is and all that He has done and is going to do in your life.

PSALM 143 – DAY 1

Show Me Where To Walk.

Let me hear of your unfailing love each morning, for I am trusting you. Show me where to walk, for I give myself to you. – Psalm 143:8 NLT

Prayer is an interesting activity. When we pray, we are oftentimes expressing to God what we want done. We are sharing our solutions to our own problems. In many cases, we treat God as some kind of cosmic Genie in the sky, except this Genie doesn't limit our wishes to just three. We can go to Him on a constant basis with requests of all kinds. Or so it would seem. But the reality is that prayer requires an understanding of who God is and the nature of His character. To ask God to do something that is not in His nature or that goes against His will would be ridiculous. But we do it all the same. God wants us to express our needs to Him, but I am not so sure that God needs help with the solution. Our prayers should be an expression of our trust and dependence on God. We go to Him because we know that He is the only one who can help. And He will help, but on His own terms and according to His own timing.

I find it interesting that David prayed quite openly and honestly with God in this psalm. He shared that he was surrounded by enemies. He told God about his struggle with depression and his being paralyzed by fear. He asked God for rescue. He asked Him to preserve his life and bring him out of his distress. He even asked God to silence his enemies and to destroy all his foes. But the more enlightening thing was that David seemed to keep His requests consistent with what he knew about God. He appealed to God's mercy. He asked God to answer because he knew God to be faithful and righteous. He knew that nothing he was asking of God was too great for Him, because he had heard about all the great things God had done in the past. He knew that his God was loving and would listen to him when he called to Him. Along with prayer for his problems, David asks God to "let me hear of your unfailing love each morning for I am trusting in you" (Psalm 143:8 NLT). What an interesting choice of words. He seems to be asking God to preserve him through the night and cause him to wake up to a renewed recognition of God's unfailing love and mercy. He will "hear" of God's love each morning. Others will be talking about it because God's intervention in David's life will be visible for all to see. It will be clear to all that this was a "God-thing." Because David is trusting in God. Then David asks God to show him where to walk. He isn't asking for literal directions, but is asking God to show him the manner in which he should live his daily life. He wants to know how to be a good king, a righteous father, a godly husband. He goes on to ask God to "teach me to do your will, for you are my God. May your gracious Spirit lead me forward on a firm footing" (Psalm 143:10 NLT). He is asking God to train him to obey. David wasn't just asking God to do things for him, he was passionate about learning to do what pleases God. He wanted to live a life in obedience to and in dependence upon God. Is that what you want? Is that what you pray and long for. David wanted rescue so that he could serve God. He wanted relief from trials and troubles, so he could spend more time worshiping and less time worrying. But he also knew that God would use those very same trials and troubles to reveal Himself to David through the display of His power, presence, love, mercy, and faithfulness. David trusted God. Do you?

Father, it is so easy for me to just come to You with my requests, but fail to want to get to know You. I want to hear of your unfailing love every morning. I want to wake up to a renewed realization of Your mercy and grace each day. I want You to teach me to do Your will, not mine. I want You to show me how to live my life in increasing obedience to and dependence upon You. You could give me all I ask for, but if I miss out on knowing You, I gain nothing. Amen

PSALM 143 – DAY 2

A Prayer For Dedication, Not Just Deliverance.
Based on Psalm 143

Hear my prayer, O Lord,
Listen attentively to my cries for help!
Answer because of Your faithfulness and righteousness.
Whatever You do, don't pass judgment on me,
Because there's not a man alive who could pass that test.
I am calling to You because my enemies constantly pursue me,
They grind my life into the ground, forcing me to live in the dark like a dead man.
As a result, my spirit is weak within me, my heart is barren and lonely.
But I can recall the past, and I think about all those things You have done;
I reflect on all the things You have done with Your hands.
So I reach out to You, my soul thirsts for You, like dry land longs for rain.
Please answer me quickly, O Lord, because my spirit is fading fast,
Don't turn Your back on me or I am as good as dead.
Let me tell others about Your unfailing love when I wake up in the morning,
Because I trust in You.
Show me the way in which You want me to live my life,
Because I am bearing my soul to You.
Rescue me from my enemies O Lord,
I run to You for protection.
Teach me to do what pleases You, because You are my God;
By Your good Spirit, lead me to a place marked by righteousness.
For the sake of Your reputation, revive me!
For the sake of Your righteousness, deliver my soul out of trouble.
And for the sake of Your unfailing love, destroy my enemies,
Put an end to all those who harass my soul,
Because I am Your servant.

PSALM 143 – DAY 3

Write Psalm 143 in your own words or write a psalm of your own. Be honest and open. Don't be afraid to tell God how you feel, but also include praise for who He is and all that He has done and is going to do in your life.

PSALM 144 – DAY 1

Who Are We Compared To You?

O Lord, what are human beings that you should notice them, mere mortals that you should think about them? – Psalm 144:3 NLT

Perspective can be an illusive thing. It is so easy to have a one-dimensional view of life and the circumstances surrounding it. We can end up seeing things from our point of view alone, and lose sight of reality. We can easily view ourselves as somehow special, our talents as truly unique, and our inherent value as greater than it really is. God provides perspective to life. He is to be the focal point to all of life and all meaning. He is the creator and sustainer of life. The world exists for Him, not the other way around. He is one who came up with the idea of humanity and then brought it about. David was blown away that this all-powerful God would even bother to waste a single second dealing with the likes of him. *The Message* paraphrases verse three quite clearly and frankly: "I wonder why you care, GOD – why do you bother with us at all?"[18]

David had a healthy perspective on life because he had an accurate view of God. He understood the greatness of God and the pitifully powerless condition of man. David lived dependent upon God – gladly and willingly. He viewed God as his rock – his source of stability and strength. He saw God as his personal trainer and reliable ally. When David ran into trouble, it was to God David ran for help, hope and healing. He didn't get too full of himself or allow his position, possessions or power to warp his perspective on life. He knew he needed God – at all times and in every way. All his strength came from God. All his victories were due to God. His rescue from trouble was totally up to God. His success or failure was in God's hands. His present prosperity and future posterity were up to God. Which is why he could say, "Yes, joyful are those who live like this! Joyful indeed are those whose God is the Lord" (Psalm 144:15 NLT). Living with a clear

---

[18] Eugene Peterson, *The Message*, NavPress Publishing Group, http://www.messagebible.com

perspective of God and life is essential to experiencing joy. When we understand just who God is, we will gladly place all our hope in Him, and refuse to see ourselves as more than what we are – mere mortals. A God-focused perspective can bring peace even in the midst of difficulty, hope in the face of heartache, and confidence even when surrounded by confusion and chaos. A healthy perspective of God gives us a healthy view of life.

Father, it is amazing that You, the God of the universe, would take time to even think about me, a mere man. But You do. You created me, care for me, sent Your Son to die for me and You have a plan that includes me. You are great, powerful, holy, sinless, righteous, and yet You choose to care for me. Thank You! Amen

PSALM 144 – DAY 2

It's Good To Know God.
Based on Psalm 144

I get down on my knees in celebration of the Lord, my rock,
He personally trains me, equipping me to do battle.
He is who I turn to for mercy, protection, refuge, deliverance from trouble,
He is my shield, and I confidently trust Him to subdue my enemies in battle.
Lord, what is man, that You bother to even acknowledge his existence?
Or the nations, that You give them any consideration at all?
Man is like a wisp of wind to You, his days are like a shadow that vanishes before
*   Your eyes.*
Lower heaven and come down, touch the mountains and make them erupt!
Send lightning, scattering the bolts around like arrows of destruction.
Reach down from on high, deliver me from the deep water, from the hands of pagan
*   nations,*
Whose words are full of lies and whose actions are always deceitful.
I will make up a brand new song celebrating You, O God!
I will sing praises to You using my favorite instrument.
I will sing of the salvation You bring to kings,
How You delivered me, David, Your servant, from the sword.
Separate me and deliver me from these foreign nations,
From all their lies and deception.
That our sons may grow to full height, like a plant,
That our daughters may be like corner stones in a beautiful palace.
That our storehouses may be full, that our sheep may multiply, filling our pastures.
That our oxen will be strong to do labor, our walls will keep us safe, and our people will
*   stay content.*
People who find themselves in those circumstances will be happy,
But their happiness will be because God is their Lord!

PSALMS 144 – DAY 3

Write Psalm 144 in your own words or write a psalm of your own. Be honest and open. Don't be afraid to tell God how you feel, but also include praise for who He is and all that He has done and is going to do in your life.

PSALM 145 – DAY 1

Sharing What We Know About God.

Let each generation tell its children of your mighty acts; let them proclaim your power. –
Psalm 145:4 NLT

We have come to the last of the psalms of David. Our goal has been to
discover the character of God through the pen of David. We hoped to see
what David understood about his God and how it impacted the way he
lived his life. And Psalm 145 seems like a perfect way to wrap up this study
of David's works. In it, David praises the greatness of God. He says, "I will
praise you every day; yes, I will praise you forever. Great is the Lord! He is
most worthy of praise! No one can measure his greatness" (Psalm 145:2-3
NLT). David is blown away by the greatness of God and wants everyone to
know. He is not content to internalize his thoughts about God and he
expects everyone to "share the story of your wonderful goodness" (Psalms
145:7 NLT). David's praise of God was not merely academic. What he
knew about God, he knew from experience. He had seen these attributes or
characteristics of God lived out in his own life, day after day. He had seen
God's power, experienced His mercy and grace, felt His compassion,
witnessed His mighty acts with his own eyes, and learned that God was
always right in everything he does. David knew what the Scriptures had to
say about God, but his awareness of God's unfailing love, truthfulness,
faithfulness, righteousness, compassion, mercy and grace came from his
own personal interactions with God in daily life.

When David wrote, "Let each generation tell its children of your mighty
acts; let them proclaim your power" (Psalm 145:4 NLT), he wasn't
suggesting that they simply recount and retell the stories they had heard
from their parent's experiences in the wilderness. Many of us can tell stories
from the Bible that illustrate God's greatness, but how many of us can
share personal encounters with God that speak of His goodness, greatness,
love, and power? There is a huge difference between knowing *about*
someone and getting to really *know* someone. I may know a lot about
Abraham Lincoln, but it all comes from books and from the perspective of

others. But I know my wife. I know her because I have spent time with her and our lives are deeply interactive and entwined. We spend time together talking, sharing, interfacing, and impacting the lives of one another. The same should be true of my relationship with God. Praise for God should be personal and intimate. It should come from experience. David had come to know God because he had spent time with God. He had watched God work in and around his life, caring for him, providing for him, protecting him, correcting him, and revealing Himself to him. David had a lot for which to praise God. When he spoke of God's wonderful goodness, mighty acts, awe-inspiring deeds, unfailing love and greatness, he was speaking from first-hand experience. He knew what he was talking about. And nobody could argue with him. So what will we have to tell the next generation concerning the mighty acts and power of God? What stories will we tell to illustrate our understanding of His greatness and goodness? Our lack of stories are not a reflection on God or proof of His absence in our lives, but are simply an indication of our lack of dependence on Him. We have little to praise Him for because we have given Him few opportunities to work in our lives. We have become self-sufficient and have attempted to run our own lives according to our own plans. But David reminds us, "The Lord is close to all who call on him, yes, to all who call on him in truth. He grants the desires of those who fear him; he hears their cries for help and rescues them. The Lord protects all those who love him" (Psalm 145:18-20 NLT).

Father, may we truly have something great to share with the next generation. May we have stories to tell of your greatness and goodness because we have learned to wait on and rely on You. Amen

PSALM 145 – DAY 2

I Can't Stop Thinking About God.
Based on Psalm 145

I will hold You in high esteem, my God and my King,
And I will bow in reverence to Your reputation forever!
I will bend my knees in praise to you every day,
I will boast of Your reputation forever and ever.
You are great, O Lord, and extremely praiseworthy.
The true extent of Your greatness is beyond our comprehension.
One generation will praise Your works to the next,
And tell them of Your strength.
I will speak of the incredible splendor of Your majesty,
And of Your extraordinary works.
They will tell of Your fear-inducing, awe-inspiring acts,
And I will recount Your greatness.
They'll overflow with memories of Your great goodness,
And be overcome by Your righteousness.
You are gracious and compassionate,
Slow to get angry and overflowing with mercy.
You show Your goodness to everyone and extend mercy to Your entire creation.
Everything You've made will end up praising You, O Lord,
And those who are faithful to You will bow down before You.
They will talk about the glory of Your reign over them and of Your great power.
They will make known to the next generation Your might acts,
And the glory of living under Your righteous rule.
Yours is a kingdom that will never end, and Your rule outlasts the generations.
You support all who fall and lift up all who are bent down and burdened.
Everyone looks to You and You provide what they need at just the right time.
You open Your hand and satisfy the needs of every living creature.
You are right in everything that You do, and always holy.
You are never far from those who call on You, who call on You in faithfulness.
You will satisfy those who fear You, hearing their cry and rescuing them.
All those who love You, You will keep safe, but those who hate You will be destroyed.

I will declare publicly my thanksgiving to You,
So that all mankind might bless Your holy name forever.

PSALMS 145 – DAY 3

Write Psalm 145 in your own words or write a psalm of your own. Be honest and open. Don't be afraid to tell God how you feel, but also include praise for who He is and all that He has done and is going to do in your life.